This book is dedicated to friendship

Thank you to the charming gardeners who
make our souls blossom

RESILIENCE

How to cope when everything around you keeps changing

Liggy Webb

Cover design: Binary & The Brain

Registered office
Capstone Publishing Ltd. (A Wiley Company), John Wiley and Sons Ltd, The Atrium, Southern Gate, Chichester, West Sussex, PO19 8SQ, United Kingdom

For details of our global editorial offices, for customer services and for information about how to apply for permission to reuse the copyright material in this book please see our website at www.wiley.com.

Wiley publishes in a variety of print and electronic formats and by print-on-demand. Some material included with standard print versions of this book may not be included in e-books or in print-on-demand. If this book refers to media such as a CD or DVD that is not included in the version you purchased, you may download this material at http://booksupport.wiley.com. For more information about Wiley products, visit www.wiley.com.

Designations used by companies to distinguish their products are often claimed as trademarks. All brand names and product names used in this book and on its cover are trade names, service marks, trademark or registered trademarks of their respective owners. The publisher and the book are not associated with any product or vendor mentioned in this book. None of the companies referenced within the book have endorsed the book.

Limit of Liability/Disclaimer of Warranty: While the publisher and author have used their best efforts in preparing this book, they make no representations or warranties with the respect to the accuracy or completeness of the contents of this book and specifically disclaim any implied warranties of merchantability or fitness for a particular purpose. It is sold on the understanding that the publisher is not engaged in rendering professional services and neither the publisher nor the author shall be liable for damages arising herefrom. If professional advice or other expert assistance is required, the services of a competent professional should be sought.

Library of Congress Cataloging-in-Publication Data
Webb, Liggy.
   Resilience : how to cope when everything around you keeps changing / Liggy Webb.
      1 online resource.
   Includes index.
   Description based on print version record and CIP data provided by publisher; resource not viewed.
      ISBN 978-0-85708-417-0 (pdf) – ISBN 978-0-85708-384-5 (epub) – ISBN 978-0-85708-386-9 (mobi) – ISBN 978-0-85708-387-6 (pbk.)   1. Resilience (Personality trait).   2. Adjustment (Psychology)   3. Change (Psychology)   I. Title.
   BF698.35.R47
   155.2'4–dc23
                              2012049066

A catalogue record for this book is available from the British Library.

ISBN 978–0-857–08387–6 (paperback) ISBN 978–0-857–08386–9 (ebk)
ISBN 978–0-857–08384–5 (ebk) ISBN 978–0-857–08417–0 (ebk)

Set in 11/14 pt Myriad Pro by Toppan Best-set Premedia Limited

Printed in Great Britain by TJ International Ltd, Padstow, Cornwall, UK

CONTENTS

An introduction to resilience   ix
How resilient are you?   xix

1. **Take a journey of self-discovery**   **1**
2. **See the glass half full**   **17**
3. **Take emotional control**   **31**
4. **Change for the better**   **47**
5. **Cope well with conflict**   **61**
6. **Embrace probortunities**   **75**
7. **Look after yourself**   **89**
8. **Make connections**   **103**
9. **Keep going**   **117**
10. **Create a vision**   **133**

Desiderata – A creed for life   147
Resilience materials   151
Top 20 survival songs   161
Useful resources   163
Acknowledgements   169
About the author   171
Index   173

*It is not the critic who counts; not the man who points out
how the strong man stumbles, or where the doer of
deeds could have done them better.*

*The credit belongs to the man who is actually in the arena, whose
face is marred by dust and sweat and blood; who strives valiantly;
who errs, who comes short again and again, because there is no
effort without error and shortcoming; but who does actually strive
to do the deeds; who knows great enthusiasms, the great devotions;
who spends himself in a worthy cause; who at the best knows
in the end the triumph of high achievement, and who at
the worst, if he fails, at least fails while daring greatly,
so that his place shall never be with those cold and
timid souls who neither know victory nor defeat.*

*For those who have had to fight for it,
life has truly a flavour the protected shall never know.*

From a speech given by Theodore Roosevelt
on the 23 April 1910, at the Sorbonne in Paris

AN INTRODUCTION TO RESILIENCE

Our greatest glory is not in never falling,
but in rising every time we fall.

Confucius

Have you ever felt sometimes as if you would like to stop the world and get off for a while, just to have a little rest, recover and make sense of it all? In the increasingly demanding and changing world that we live in, it is so easy sometimes to become overwhelmed and feel as if you are sinking.

At some point, everyone experiences varying degrees of setbacks. Some of these challenges might be relatively minor and others may have a major impact. How you deal with these problems can play a major part in the ultimate outcome and also your long-term psychological well-being.

Resilient people are able to utilize their skills and strengths to cope and recover from the knockbacks and challenges, which could well include illness, job loss, financial problems, natural disasters, relationship break-ups or the death of someone you love.

If you lack resilience you may become overwhelmed by these experiences and simply fall apart. You may find yourself dwelling on your problems and using unhealthy coping mechanisms to deal with the pain and heartache.

It would be fair to say that some individuals do indeed have personality traits that help them remain calm in the face of adversity. Others may well react more emotionally and dramatically. We will, of course, all react differently to trauma and stress in our lives. Some people take a more stoic approach and keep their feelings hidden; others may become more expressive and emotional. Different personalities tend to process information in a variety of ways and your reaction will be part of your coping mechanism.

The key, however, is the end result. It isn't necessarily a question of how far you fall, but how high you can bounce back; sometimes, maybe, even bigger, better and stronger as a result of the experience.

Like the boomerang on the cover of the book, you show true resilience by returning from each experience relatively unscathed and ready to face positively the next challenge that life may throw your way.

What you need to avoid is becoming a 'Doomerang', returning from each experience loaded with negative baggage, resentments and pain that could well haunt you for the rest of your life and make the next situation even harder to deal with.

Resilient people do not allow adversity to drain their resolve. They find a way to pick themselves up, dust themselves off and keep going, with a strong belief that things can, and will, get better.

Resilience comes from the Latin word *resilio*, which means 'to jump back'. Some people describe resilience as the ability to *bend* instead of *breaking* under pressure, or the ability to persevere and adapt when faced with challenges. The same abilities also help us to be more open and willing to take on new opportunities. In this way, resilience is more than just survival, it is also about letting go and learning to grow.

Throughout this book you will find that some of the greatest examples of people who cope exceptionally well with adversity are those who adopt a positive mental attitude.

As a total advocate of positivity, I would like to share with you a very recent story about resilience which involves my own family.

A PERSONAL STORY OF RESILIENCE

To set the scene, my parents have been together for over 60 years, married for nearly 58, and have three children. Certainly they have had their share of challenges and heartache; however, they are both strong, positive people who cope amazingly well with whatever life throws at them.

Three years ago my father started feeling breathless and tired. As a very fit 75-year-old, who sailed every weekend and went to gym five times a week, it was thought that perhaps he was overdoing it. He went to see his doctor who said that he had a heart murmur and sent him to see a consultant at the local hospital. This was diagnosed as a moderate condition.

Last year, however, it was discovered that he had severe thickening of the aortic valve and, after an angiogram, he was told that he needed a quadruple bypass as well as a valve replacement. The situation was diagnosed as severe and he was put on a waiting list, with his health deteriorating on a daily basis. He was given strict instructions to do no more sailing, no more gym and to remain wrapped in cotton wool until after the operation.

For someone who was used to an active life this was very challenging. Each day he waited with no communication of when the operation would be. Bouts of anxiety and depression become frequent as his life was put on hold. To watch my parents go through this ordeal alone was heart wrenching as they were rendered helpless.

One year later, he was finally given an operation date. The news, when it finally came was seemingly akin to winning the lottery! The whole family was tremendously relieved.

The evening before the operation, my mother and I took my father into hospital and I watched them say their goodbyes. Knowing the severity and the risk of the operation, I have to say, I struggled to hold it together. After 60 years of being together they knew there was a chance, as with any major operation, that this could be the last time they saw each other.

Knowing it was a six-hour operation, I tried to keep my mother busy as we both waited with our hearts in our mouths. All we wanted to do was call to be able to hear that everything had gone well. Four hours later, the phone rang and I answered it, my mouth dry with anticipation and fear. It was a surreal experience to hear my father's voice on the end of the line.

'Well it's like this', his ghostlike voice whispered down the phone line. 'I was all ready to go into theatre. They'd prepared me. Put my gown on. I'd even had a Mexican!' (I didn't feel it was appropriate to correct him at that point.) 'And then they said that I was going to be discharged because they didn't have any critical care beds left!'

My mother and I immediately went to see my father and we found him sitting on the end of his hospital bed looking somewhat bewildered, trying to make sense of this surreal situation. Despite their extraordinary efforts to remain calm I could see the fear in my parents' eyes as they imagined being flung back into the bureaucracy of waiting lists, and it all seemed almost too unbearable to imagine. No one was able to give us any information, only that my father should return home and wait for the next available slot which could be days, weeks or months.

We returned home and I watched my parents muster a huge amount of resilience as they both discussed how they would deal with the situation. They realized that the situation was out of their control and they made a pact to be calm and patient and that things would be resolved if they remained positive.

After being home for about two hours the telephone rang. Half-expecting it to be a concerned relative, I answered it. I was told that my father should return immediately to the hospital as a critical care bed had become available and my father would be operated on the next day. Repacking his bag we traipsed back to the hospital. This I am sure you can imagine would be an ordeal for anyone let alone two people near to eighty!

We left my father that evening and called later to see if he was settled. He said he had spoken to the Sister on the ward who said he was doing very well and she was surprised at how positively he had dealt with it all.

Apparently he had said to the Sister that his daughter wrote books about being positive and he had then proceeded to tell her that he had PMT.

'Oh sir', the Sister had said 'I think you mean PMA'.

'No', he had apparently told her quite adamantly. 'I think under the circumstances I am entitled to have PMT!'

The next period of time was an even more nerve-wracking ordeal because, after the operation, my father remained in a coma, unable to come off the life support machine. Eventually, after a week, he came out of critical care and with all the drugs and tubes that had been attached to him he was convinced that he was on the moon!

My father is now recovering very well and with the support of my mother and various health professionals he is back on his feet and enjoying his latest passion of model yacht racing. He says he feels he has a new lease of life and most certainly seems to have bounced back even better than before, despite having been through a somewhat traumatic ordeal.

As you will see, I take courage from other people's stories as well as my own experiences and, dotted throughout this book, are some other enlightening and inspiring examples. I have changed a few names where appropriate to protect privacy. Some people, it seems, have more than their fair share of pain. Certainly some of the stories in this book will demonstrate this. However, those stories have reaffirmed my belief that it is not what happens to you in life, it is how you respond and deal with the situation that matters.

In my previous book, *How to be Happy*, my aim was to help people to feel better about themselves and their lives. This book, however, goes a little more deeply into helping people to handle the trials, tribulations and curve balls that life throws at us from time to time. I have outlined ten key strategies for developing resilience; with information, tips and techniques so that you can develop your own coping mechanism and take better control of your life.

1. TAKE A JOURNEY OF SELF-DISCOVERY

Self-awareness and self-confidence play an essential role in helping you to cope with stress and recover from difficult events. Understanding yourself is the first port of call and, after that, reminding yourself of your strengths and accomplishments is key. Becoming more confident about your ability to respond and deal with crises is a great way to build resilience for the future. Challenges can be stepping stones or stumbling blocks. It's just a matter of how you view them and how much faith you have in yourself to overcome them.

2. SEE THE GLASS HALF FULL

Staying positive during dark periods can be difficult and it is important to maintain a hopeful outlook. Being an optimist does not mean being naive and ignoring the problem. It means understanding that setbacks are transient and that you have the skills and abilities to combat the challenges you face. There is a huge risk when something difficult arises that you fall into the pessimistic trap of believing that everything is doom and gloom. So much of resilience is about how you choose to react to each situation, and an optimistic perspective will most certainly lead you in a more positive direction.

3. TAKE EMOTIONAL CONTROL

Being emotionally aware and recognizing how potentially you can react in certain situations will help you to exert more self-control. It will also help you to be more considerate with regards to how your reactions can affect other people. High emotion can be quite exhausting so managing emotions during any ordeal will help you to focus your energy where it's best placed. People who have better emotional awareness and understand their own emotions have been shown to be far more resilient.

4. CHANGE FOR THE BETTER

Being positive about change is a really good approach. You may not be able to control or change circumstances; however, you can absolutely change your attitude towards them so you are far more in control than you think. Flexibility is an essential part of being able to manage change and, by learning how to be more adaptable, you will be much better equipped to respond to any life crisis you experience. Resilient people often utilize these events as an opportunity to branch out in new directions. While some people may be crushed by abrupt changes, highly resilient individuals are able to adapt and thrive.

5. COPE WELL WITH CONFLICT

Conflict is an inevitable part of life. We all have different personalities, and along with those go belief systems, values, perspectives, likes and dislikes. Some conflict can be difficult and, at times, unsettling – especially if you take it personally and are very sensitive. The outcome of conflict, however, can be very positive. It can help you to create new ideas, learn from others, understand yourself better, see different perspectives and improve your own communication. Learning how to cope with and manage conflict is a very important life skill in the increasingly diverse world that we live in.

6. EMBRACE PROBORTUNITIES

The word *probortunity* is a hybrid between the word 'problem' and 'opportunity' and looks at the concept of taking every problem situation and seeking out the opportunity. It works on the premise that in every crisis situation an opportunity will arise and there will be some benefit. It is a useful approach to problems and helps you come at them from a positive angle. Developing a good set of problem-solving skills is a valuable toolkit to equip yourself with and knowing what practical steps to take will give you confidence when you are faced with adversity.

7. LOOK AFTER YOURSELF

When you are feeling traumatized, stressed and upset, it can be all too easy to neglect your own well-being. Losing your appetite, overeating, not exercising, not getting enough sleep, drinking too much alcohol, not drinking enough water, driving yourself too hard, are all common reactions to a crisis situation. This is the time when you need to work on building your self-nurturance skills, especially when you are troubled. Making time to invest into your well-being will boost your overall health and resilience and you will be better equipped to be face life's challenges.

8. MAKE CONNECTIONS

Building and sustaining a strong network of supportive friends, family and work colleagues will act as a protective factor during times of crisis. It is important to have people you trust and can confide in. Whilst simply talking about a situation with a friend or loved one will not necessarily make troubles go away, it will allow you to share your feelings, gain support, receive feedback and come up with possible solutions to your problems. Listening to other people's experiences can be really useful too and, although we can't always learn from others mistakes, there will certainly be some good advice out there.

9. KEEP GOING

Winston Churchill summed this up perfectly: 'If you are going through hell, keep going.' There is a lot be said for picking yourself up, dusting yourself off and carrying on. Being resilient is about the ability to bounce back and get on with life. The key is to think of each setback or upset as a stepping stone – and it is really important to be able to do this as quickly as possible. Letting go of the angst that you experience too is very important rather than carrying lots of negative baggage with you that will just weigh you down and make the journey ahead more difficult.

10. CREATE A VISION

In times of crisis, or when you are feeling low, it is good to hold on to your dream and not lose sight of the fact that you can always have something to look forward to. There are lots of benefits to creating a vision and setting goals. First and foremost, they help you to develop clarity which is the first step to helping you achieve what you want in life. Goals unlock your positive mind and release energies and ideas for success and achievement. Without goals, you simply drift and flow on the currents of life. With goals, you fly like an arrow, straight and true to your target. Setting goals gives you direction, purpose, focus and, most important of all, hope.

At the end of each chapter there are also some reflection exercises where you can examine your own needs and set out a personal action plan to ensure that you truly benefit from this book. Knowledge is much more valuable when you put it to good use.

This book is written with the intention of providing you with some fundamental strategies that will help you to navigate some of the challenges you may face in your life. It is has been designed to be an easy and accessible read so you won't find a huge amount of science and theory. It cuts through unnecessary complexity and will provide you with simple solutions to get back on track and trust that tomorrow has every possibility of being a brighter, better day.

Liggy Webb

Learn from yesterday, live for today, hope for tomorrow.

Albert Einstein

HOW RESILIENT ARE YOU?

Before you start to read this book, it will be interesting for you to see just how resilient you are. This quiz will take you a few minutes to complete and will give you some indication of how you are doing.

Rate yourself from 1 to 5 on the following: (1 = very little, 5 = very strong)

In a crisis or chaotic situation, I calm myself and focus on taking useful actions.	1	2	3	4	5
I'm usually optimistic. I see difficulties as temporary and expect to overcome them.	1	2	3	4	5
I can tolerate high levels of ambiguity and uncertainty about situations.	1	2	3	4	5
I adapt quickly to new developments. I'm good at bouncing back from difficulties.	1	2	3	4	5
I'm playful. I find the humour in rough situations, and can laugh at myself.	1	2	3	4	5

	1	2	3	4	5
I'm able to recover emotionally from losses and setbacks. I have friends I can talk with. I can express my feelings to others and ask for help. Feelings of anger, loss and discouragement don't last long.	1	2	3	4	5
I feel self-confident, appreciate myself. and have a healthy concept of who I am.	1	2	3	4	5
I'm curious. I ask questions. I want to know how things work. I like to try new ways of doing things.	1	2	3	4	5
I learn valuable lessons from my experiences and from the experiences of others.	1	2	3	4	5
I'm good at solving problems. I can use analytical logic, be creative, or use practical common sense.	1	2	3	4	5
I'm good at making things work well. I'm often asked to lead groups and projects.	1	2	3	4	5
I'm very flexible. I feel comfortable with my paradoxical complexity. I'm optimistic and pessimistic, trusting and cautious, unselfish and selfish, and so forth.	1	2	3	4	5
I'm always myself, but I've noticed that I'm different in different situations.	1	2	3	4	5

I prefer to work without a written job description. I'm more effective when I'm free to do what I think is best in each situation.	1	2	3	4	5
I "read" people well and trust my intuition.	1	2	3	4	5
I'm a good listener. I have good empathy skills.	1	2	3	4	5
I'm non-judgmental about others and adapt to people's different personality styles.	1	2	3	4	5
I'm very durable. I hold up well during tough times. I have an independent spirit underneath my cooperative way of working with others.	1	2	3	4	5
I've been made stronger and better by difficult experiences.	1	2	3	4	5
I've converted misfortune into good luck and found benefits in bad experiences.	1	2	3	4	5
Add your Total					

Grand Total

Scoring

Over 85 – You demonstrate high levels of resilience
65–85 – You show the ability to be resilient in most situations
50–65 – You can cope in some situations
40–50 – You really struggle to be resilient
Under 40 – You really need to work on developing resilience

Resiliency Quiz reprinted with permission by Practical Psychology Press. From The Resiliency Center website, based upon *The Resiliency Advantage* by Al Siebert, PhD (2006, Berrett-Koehler).

TAKE A
JOURNEY OF
SELF-DISCOVERY

Promise me you'll always remember: You're braver than you believe, and stronger than you seem, and smarter than you think.

Christopher Robin to Pooh (by A. A. Milne)

Whenever something happens in your life that may result in loss or change and pain, in whatever guise, something very special can occur at the same time. You are given an opportunity to reassess your position in life and to learn something new and potentially empowering.

Resilience very often is referred to as the ability to bounce back from adversity. The question to ask is:

Do I want to bounce back to where I am right now?

It may be that, through the apparent process of upset and upheaval, you can move your life into a far better position than it is at the moment. The situation that may be causing your current anxiety may well be a springboard for you to make some positive changes that you would never have thought of before.

Reassessing the relationship you have with yourself is very important because this will be the time that you need to tap into all your inner strength and work on any weakness. There will, of course, be people around you who can support you; however, you are ultimately your own salvation and developing your coping ability is essential to survival.

Feeling positive about who and what you are will provide you with a solid foundation and developing a healthy amount of self-respect and self-worth is a good place to start.

BE YOUR PERSONAL BEST

It is important first of all to take personal responsibility for being the best that you can be. So often it is easy to compare yourself to others and, if you do this, you run the danger of engendering two emotions: one of vanity or one of bitterness, because there will always be people you come across who you perceive as better or worse off than yourself. It is also pointless to benchmark yourself against others. Using yourself as your own benchmark is far more constructive.

My sister Jacky Pearson is a wonderfully talented watercolour artist who lives in New Zealand. When I first started writing, I lacked confidence in my ability to be as good as other writers, and she said that she had felt the same about her art. She decided one day, however, that she would no longer allow herself to do this, and her focus and ambition would be about being a better artist than she had been the year before, and use this as her goal and herself as her own benchmark. This was a great piece of advice, and certainly helps take away the weight of pressure that we can so unnecessarily put upon ourselves.

Just Be You!

Persons of high self-esteem are not driven to make themselves superior to others; they do not seek to prove their value by measuring themselves against a comparative standard. Their joy is being who they are, not in being better than someone else.

Nathaniel Branden

Imagine having no one to compare yourself with except yourself. What a sense of relief this would bring. You wouldn't have to give yourself a hard time about not performing as well as your colleagues at work. You wouldn't have to worry about not looking like the most attractive person with the smartest mind or having the most important job role and the biggest pay packet. You wouldn't have to worry about your body not being the fittest or most beautiful and most sexy.

All you would need to ask yourself is:

- Did I do this better than I did it last time?

- Have I moved forward in my own definition of success?

- Am I feeling content?

- Am I doing my best for my health?

- Do I have an attractive mind and healthy interactions with other people?

In Neuro-Linguistic Programming, broad distinctions are made between predominantly internally-referenced people who are generally better at using their own referencing to measure their success and those who are more externally-referenced, who look for reassurance and confirmation of their abilities from others. Externally-referenced people are more likely to make comparisons with other people as a kind of self-affirmation, but no one lives in a vacuum and everyone has some kind of referencing system to people outside of themselves.

We all have an actual or imagined audience to our lives that gives our actions meaning. One of the first steps in improving self-esteem is to learn where we currently position ourselves on the line of continuum between being internally-referenced and externally-referenced. Nobody is entirely one type or the other and different patterns will play out with different people at different times. In the workplace, for example, the quality and nature of the relationships we have with colleagues will be coloured by the degree to which we are externally-referenced and the number and strength of comparisons we make in relation to job roles, personality types and status.

Our behaviour will be determined by these perceptions and, for example, a conversation with a team member might be very different from a conversation with a line manager. The outcome of the interaction cannot be viewed in isolation from our perceptions of who we are, the boundaries of our role, who our colleague is, the boundaries of their role and the value of our role compared to our colleague's role.

In addition, the perceptions we have and comparisons we make will be based on what we see and hear. However, we see and hear only a small range of other people's behaviour and we need to take this into account when we examine our perceptions.

To pull all of this together, we are making assessments based on a small chunk of information that is internally processed through a system coloured by our own perceptions of self, role, status and personality type! It is no wonder that many people find success a difficult concept to grasp and find it easier to use other people's measures of success than find their own!

The most powerful place on the continuum is in the middle: having a faith in your own perception and judgement but still being open and receptive to others' feedback.

So, in addition to recognizing your referencing systems, and to fully understand personal success, you will need to take a good, deep look into the essence of your being and see what it is that makes you who you are.

ASK YOURSELF THE FOLLOWING QUESTIONS

- What qualities make me feel good about myself?
- What can I offer to the world around me?

- What is my personal success gauge?

- What is my own definition of happiness?

You can then accept that your definition of success might look completely different from someone else's. What you think of you is the most important opinion.

The more clarity you have around your definition, the more you will have demonstrated personal honesty and the creative imagination to think outside of other people's referencing systems. This will help you to take responsibility for your own perceptions and definition of reality. This then will become the place that you will want to bounce back from any adversity that you may have to deal with.

WHAT VALUE DO YOU GIVE YOURSELF?

Something else to consider is how much you value yourself. This will provide you with something to think about.

- A bar of iron costs £5
- Made into horseshoes it can be worth about £20
- Made into needles it can increase its value to £3500
- Made into balance springs for watches, its value can leap to £250,000.

Remember, your own value is determined also by what you are able to make of yourself.

We are all people in progress which is very exciting because we have the ability to make improvements every day of our lives and keep adding value to our pot of self-worth.

Appreciating and valuing yourself is the most important component of self-love. However that sounds, it is hugely important, because if you don't love yourself, how would you even begin to expect anyone else to?

Many years ago I met a young woman called Megan, who made a huge impression upon me, whilst I was working on a community project for homeless people in North London. I was so impressed by her vitality and passion for life. She was a beautiful and vibrant person who always wore beautiful bright scarves and had a great sense of humour. She also had a very deep scar that ran from her forehead across her eye to her lip and she seemed totally unselfconscious about it even though people used to stare at her. As I got to know her, I realized that she had worked very hard to cultivate her attitude and indeed her sense of self-worth.

Megan was born in Trinidad and came to London when she was five, with her mother and brother, to escape an abusive father. Initially they lived with the grandparents, and then moved to a council flat in Camden. Her mother soon became involved in yet another dysfunctional relationship, and Megan and her younger brother were regularly physically and mentally abused. Eventually they were taken into care after they were both subjected to a severe beating that left Megan's face badly scarred and partially sighted in her right eye.

She was frequently bullied by people who were prejudiced about her background and her apparent disfiguration. She said that she grew up with very little self-esteem and believed she was ugly and worthless. When she was fourteen she was fostered by a wonderful Irish family who helped to restore Megan's self-esteem and she became passionate about helping others with disability and trained as a school assistant to work with children with special needs.

Megan was encouraged by her foster mother Mary to see her experiences in life as something that would help her to empathize with other people who may have suffered too. If this vision remained strong, and she followed her dreams, it would inspire and encourage others to do the same.

I remember Megan telling me that when she looked in the mirror that she didn't see her scar or her challenged past. What she saw was a bright, colourful woman who was beautiful in her own right and who lived a meaningful life which meant that she added value herself which helped her to feel really good about herself.

FEAR AND DESIRE

It is important, at this point, to understand that human beings are essentially driven by fear and desire and, very often, fear can over-ride our ability to want to make changes. Fearful people get stuck in what they perceive as their safe zone and any upheaval appears insurmountable. The fear of the unknown can be quite scary and the danger sometimes is that we can allow our minds to imagine all sorts of negative outcomes. This is where you need to work at turning these situations around and focusing on what you want the outcome to be and take control of where you would like to get to.

LEARN TO TRUST

Trusting yourself and others is key and to really trust is something that requires a certain amount of confidence and also the ability to occasionally move out of your comfort zone. Being able to trust someone is a real gift; however, it is a gift that brings with it vulnerability.

Positive relationships are built on the cornerstone of trust. Sometimes it can be difficult to let go of the paranoia and fear that tends to attach itself to trust, especially if you have been hurt or let down. It may not be easy, but if you simply behave in the way that you would expect others to behave towards you, then this will help you to build this trust in yourself and others.

FEEDBACK

To understand yourself better, you will also need to be receptive to feedback – from yourself and from others – because this will help you to get a wider perspective. Sometimes people will see potential in you of which you may have no awareness whatsoever. Receiving feedback can also be challenging even if it is something I like to term as the 'food of progress'. However, like some foods, while it may be good for us, it can also be a little unpleasant to digest. However, the more you can let your guard down and open up, and the more you will see feedback as free information that can add huge value.

INVEST IN YOU

The very best investment that you can make primarily to yourself and to those around you is to invest time and energy into yourself. Sometimes people fall into the trap of being the helper to every person in their vicinity and, literally, running out of energy and losing sight of what they need themselves to be strong and healthy. This is counterproductive because when you reach burnout you are no good to anyone around you, least of all to yourself.

Taking time out each day for yourself is essential for you to take stock of who and what and how you are.

Ask yourself from time to time these three questions:

1. Who am I?

2. What am I?

3. How am I?

He who knows others is learned;
He who knows himself is wise.

Lao-tzu

BUILDING SELF-CONFIDENCE

Working on your own self-confidence is a very important part of building resilience. Below are some tips that may help you to do that.

There are many ways to develop self-confidence and what works for some may not work for another. However, here are few suggestions:

1 **Believe in yourself.** The real key to self-confidence is to believe in yourself and to trust your own views and opinions. This, at times, can be difficult, especially if you have a tendency to listen to others and benchmark yourself against what they think of you. This is, however, very dangerous and the ability to be able to establish your own inner benchmark to success is essential, as we have already covered.

2 **Like yourself.** If there is something about yourself that you do not like then do something about it. Every human being has the potential ability to take control and make positive changes. Other people can try and stop you, but only if you let them. When you look in the mirror, be proud of the person that you see, knowing that you do the best you can every day of your life and, even if you make a mistake, see it as valuable lesson learnt. Even if you make the same mistake a few times you are not always going to get everything right every time.

3 **Listen to yourself.** Tell yourself that you are confident and believe in yourself. Focus on your strengths and the positive aspects of your character and set about developing the areas that you have for potential. Be your own best friend and, above all, be really kind to yourself and make sure that you do things that nourish not deplete you.

4 **Develop good practicing.** The way a person carries themselves tells a story. People with slumped shoulders and lethargic movements display a lack of self-confidence. By practising good posture, you'll automatically feel more confident. Stand up straight, keep your head up, and make eye contact. You'll make a positive impression on others and instantly feel more alert and empowered.

5 **Develop an attitude of gratitude.** Be grateful for what you have. Set aside time each day to list mentally everything you have to be grateful for. Recall your past successes, unique skills, loving relationships, and positive momentum. You'll be amazed how much you have going for you, and motivated to take that next step towards success.

6 **Compliment other people.** When we think negatively about ourselves, we often project that feeling on to others in the form of insults and gossip. To break this cycle of negativity, get in the habit of praising other people. Refuse to engage in backstabbing office gossip and make an effort to compliment those around you. In the process, you'll become well-liked and, by looking for the best in others, you indirectly bring out the best in yourself.

7 **Speak up.** During group discussions and meetings at work, many people never speak up because they're afraid that people will judge them for saying something stupid. This fear isn't really justified. Generally, people are much more accepting than we imagine. In fact, most people are dealing with the exact same fears.

8 **Exercise.** Along the same lines as personal appearance, physical fitness has a huge effect on self-confidence. If you're out of shape, you'll feel insecure, unattractive, and less energetic. By working out, you improve your physical appearance, energize yourself, and accomplish something positive. Having the discipline to work out not only makes you feel better, it creates positive momentum that you can build on for the rest of the day.

9 **Look outwards.** Sometimes, when we are feeling low, we can become introspective and kick things around in our mind

in a way that drains our energy. This is the time when it is good to look up and outwards and start to focus on the things around us. Smile and acknowledge others, show an interest in what they are doing and what is going on. This can help you to get off your own case for a while and regain a balanced perspective.

So, in terms of ensuring that you have built the best possible platform to bounce back to, it is really important, first of all, to know and understand who you really are. You will then need to examine whether you are totally happy with who and what and how you are and, if not, you have the opportunity to make some positive changes.

You will be able to work on your self-esteem and develop your self-confidence and ensure that your personal value and sense of self-worth is the best it could possibly be. Remember YOU are your most valuable asset!

Really knowing and understanding yourself is a very important part of developing resilience. Self-awareness is a recognition of who you are and an acknowledgement of your strengths and weaknesses, your likes and dislikes. Developing self-awareness can help you to recognize when you are stressed or under pressure. It is also often a prerequisite for effective communication and interpersonal relations, as well as being critical for developing empathy for others. We will take a good look at emotions in the third chapter of this book; however, self-awareness is a vital ingredient for developing your emotional intelligence.

Being self-aware is the first step in the creation process. As you grow in self-awareness, you will understand better why you feel the way you do and why you behave the way you do in certain situations. That understanding then gives you the opportunity and freedom to change those things you would like to change about yourself and create the life that you really want, and the place you would most want to bounce back to. Without fully knowing who you are, self-acceptance and change are virtually impossible.

The journey of self-discovery can, at times, be a painful process because, when we take a good look in the metaphorical mirror, we may not always like what we see. We may well learn things about ourselves that make us afraid. However, this is where the true voyage of discovery takes place – on the crest of a wave – this is where you can begin to cast off the shackles that may hold you down and stop you from making positive progress.

Positive Steps

1 Examine the value you give yourself
2 Understand your strengths and weaknesses
3 Develop techniques to improve your self-confidence
4 Listen to yourself and others, and seek feedback
5 Be open-minded to making positive changes about yourself

Take a journey of self-discovery – Personal exercise

- Providing evidence to back this up, write down the three things that you believe are your greatest strengths.
- Do the same about the three things that you believe are your biggest weaknesses.
- Ask three people, a friend, a family member and a work colleague, to tell you what they think your three strengths and weaknesses are and ask for evidence.
- Write down five words you would like to hear if you were being described by someone else, and the reasons why.
- Make an action plan of what you are going to do each day to aspire to be the five things that you would most like to be.

It's never too late to be who you might have been

George Eliot

2

SEE THE GLASS
HALF FULL

*Even if I knew that tomorrow the world would go to pieces,
I would still plant my apple tree*

Martin Luther King

Dear Optimist and Pessimist and Realist,

While you were arguing about the glass being half empty or half full, I just wanted to let you know that I drank it.

Kind Regards

The Opportunist

As an advocate of the glass half full, I have lived my life with a firm belief that there are huge benefits to being positive and optimistic. I have had many a good debate with so-called 'realists' who have accused me of being a naive optimist. However, thinking positively is not about putting your head in the sand and being unrealistic, as some people may believe. With a positive attitude you can also recognize the negative aspects of a situation and make a conscious decision to focus instead on the hope and opportunity that is available. This releases you from getting locked in a paralyzing loop of negative emotion and allows you to bounce back from adversity and challenging experiences.

Optimism is also known to be a root cause of many life benefits. The relatively new science of *psychoneuroimmunology* looks at how our mind can influence our immune system. The theory is that you will live longer and be healthier and happier by cultivating a positive attitude toward life.

Ten good reasons for being positive and optimistic

1 Live longer and recover quicker from illness
2 Cultivate happy and successful relationships
3 Deal constructively with perceived failure
4 Be more hopeful and proactive
5 Feel more energized and motivated
6 Improve your ability to make decisions
7 Be more creative and adventurous
8 View change as an opportunity to learn and grow
9 Appreciate and enjoy life to the full
10 Bounce back quicker from adversity and knockbacks

Clearly this is not an exhaustive list and there are many more benefits to being optimistic. One of my favourite books is Nelson Mandela's autobiography *Long Walk to Freedom* and this passage of writing sums up optimism very well.

I am fundamentally an optimist. Whether that comes from nature or nurture, I cannot say. Part of being optimistic is keeping one's head pointed toward the sun, one's feet moving forward. There were many dark moments when my faith in humanity was sorely tested, but I would not and could not give myself up to despair.

Giving up, of course, is an option for anyone who faces trauma. However, it is the fighting spirit that we all possess within us that will keep us going. It can be very challenging to be optimistic at times, especially when you feel that the world is conspiring against you and you find yourself in the eye of the storm. Inevitably, we all have dark periods and it is simply not possible to control everything that happens to you. The resilience some people demonstrate in some situations never ceases to amaze me: a friend of mine, has very bravely and kindly allowed me to share her story which is heartwarming and heart wrenching in equal measure.

A few years ago, when I first moved to Cheltenham where I now live, I set up a writing group. I was keen to bring together people who share a passion for creative writing and to cultivate a relaxed, fun and social environment. Over the years, the group has evolved and now hosts a fabulous and eclectic cast of individuals who are highly talented – there really is never a dull moment!

Strong friendships have been forged and there has certainly been a fair share of success, excitement, high drama, personality clashes and, sadly, loss and illness. My friend Eleanor, who is one of the members of the writing group, gives a candid account of coping with extreme adversity and how optimism has kept her going.

A DAY CLOSER TO BEING BETTER

Just before Christmas in 2008, Eleanor – who was, at the time, a freelance consultant and in her late forties – felt a strange sensation in the back of her throat. She took a mirror and torch and could see that there was some puffiness. She went to the doctor and was prescribed with antibiotics. These had no effect and they decided to take the tonsil out and, after a biopsy, they diagnosed that she had non-Hodgkin's lymphoma (NHL) which is the fifth most common cancer in the UK.

To some extent, the cancer was not a surprise to Eleanor because she had explored the internet and had anticipated cancer as a possibility. She was told that she would receive chemotherapy and, at that time, made a decision to try to tune out her emotional response and focus on the practical steps.

To help her to mentally condition herself in preparation for what she was about to go through she focused on the following two phrases:

1 Every day is a day closer to being better.

2 I've got an illness. They are treating it and I am going to get better.

Throughout her treatment Eleanor attempted to remain strong and positive. She recalls one day, however, when she was sitting in the support centre for cancer patients waiting for treatment. Suddenly, it really hit her that she was going to lose her hair. Eleanor remembers bursting into tears, and said that losing her hair was one of the strangest sensations, with great lumps coming out in her hands as she ran a comb through it. She kept reminding herself each day that she would get better and it would grow again.

After a series of gruelling tests, including bone marrow samples and chemotherapy, it was discovered during a CT scan that, not only did Eleanor have non-Hodgkin's lymphoma, she also had large tumours on her pancreas and liver. These were neuroendocrine tumours which is a rare cancer known as the silent killer because there are few side effects or apparent indicators.

Eleanor's initial reaction was how lucky she was that the first cancer had been diagnosed – if it hadn't, she would never have known about the other cancer which would have been fatal.

Shortly after 50th birthday, Eleanor went into hospital and had an operation to remove the 4-inch tumour across her pancreas and a 2-inch tumour across her liver. With it they took a third of her liver, some of the tail of her pancreas and all of her spleen.

After the operation began the long haul to recovery and, gradually, she became stronger, joining a health program at the gym. She was determined that this experience wasn't going to change anything and began to see her recovery period as an opportunity to improve her life.

She hadn't been completely fulfilled with her life before the diagnosis as a freelance consultant. Now she had time to think. What she wanted to do was reconnect with her History of Art degree. She realized that, in her life, she had made some decisions she would have changed and had missed some golden opportunities. Eleanor decided to volunteer with the art gallery and museum in Cheltenham and approached a leading heritage organization to do some part-time, voluntary work.

A year after her annual check-up, two more tumours in the liver were discovered, which needed a further operation. Again, the recovery process began and Eleanor continued to remind herself that every day was a day closer to being better. She continued to pursue her ambitions and stayed focused and determined. A few months later she received an internship with the heritage organization.

Then, another huge knock-back occurred. On the first day of her new job she received a call to say that more cancer had been discovered and she would need to have open liver surgery. This time, however, she had the security of a job to go back to and greater support.

Eleanor has now been cleared of the initial cancer, non-Hodgkin's lymphoma, and awaits the results of the scan for the neuroendo-crine cancer. She remains hopeful and believes that everything will be OK. She has put her faith in science and has been fortunate enough to be operated on by some of the top liver surgeons in the country.

Eleanor says she feels truly fulfilled in the work she is now doing, which she may never have discovered had she not experienced her illness. New possibilities have opened up to her and she believes that an optimistic and positive outlook has kept her going.

HOW TO BE OPTIMISTIC

The antidote to negativity and pessimism is to learn to accept responsibility for your situation. The very act of taking responsi-bility cancels out any negative emotion and, by embracing respon-sibility, you will reap many rewards. The successes brought by this attitude will act as a cornerstone for self-respect, pride and residents.

It can be easy to blame others or circumstances for everything in our lives – past, present or future – and it lets us off the hook to some degree. Ultimately, however, it doesn't help us because we become a prisoner of circumstance and allow everything and everyone around us to dictate our world. The danger then is that you become a 'victim' and adopt the 'poor me' syndrome. This may work for a while because feeling sorry for yourself can take some pressure away from doing anything about it and, of course, you may get some sympathy and support from others who care about you, and who are willing to be supportive. Occasionally, we all need tea and sympathy and there is nothing wrong with that from time to time. The danger, however, is that some people cultivate a victim mentality and see everyone around them as their helper and this can be rather draining for all concerned.

There are those who may well mock the genre of 'self-help'. However, a good question to ask is 'What better kind of help is there?' Developing coping mechanisms and taking personal responsibility for your attitude will empower you and make you stronger and more resourceful.

The internal dialogue that you have will very much influence the way that you react. If you believe that everything is gloomy, the chances are that you will create that outcome and it will become a self-fulfilling prophecy.

MIND OVER MATTER

The expression *mind over matter* is so true when it comes to the way that you react to situations. When it comes to your attitude, your brain is your most valuable and important asset and how it works will determine how positive you can be and how capable you feel with regards to resilience.

Up until relatively recently, scientists could only speculate about the brain's role in defining our personalities and behaviours. There were not the advanced tools that we have now to look at the functioning of the brain, and false assumptions were made about its impact on our lives. With the advent of sophisticated brain-imaging techniques, the brain's role in behaviour is being explored and examined at a phenomenal pace and we are learning more each day, which really is incredible.

It is such an exciting and fascinating time to be around as the mysteries of the mind are unfolding and we are learning more and more about the fascinating instrument that we have in our possession: the human brain!

Your living is determined not so much by what life brings to you as by the attitude you bring to life; not so much by what happens to you as by the way your mind looks at what happens.

Khalil Gibran

Conditioning your thinking

There is one part of your brain that is important to be aware of, and plays a vital part in your ability to achieve positive outcomes and influence your way of thinking. This is known as your 'reticular activating system'.

This is a filter that takes instructions from your conscious mind and passes them on to your subconscious.

The RAS consists of a bundle of densely packed nerve cells located in the central core of the brainstem. Roughly the size of your little finger, it runs from the top of the spinal cord into the middle of your brain. This area of tightly packed fibres and cells contain nearly 70% of your brain's nerve cells.

The RAS acts as an executive secretary for your conscious mind. It is the chief gatekeeper to screen or filter the type of information that will be allowed to get through. Everything else is filtered out and you don't pay attention to those other 'messages' because they are screened out.

(Continued)

There are some interesting points about your reticular activating system that make it an essential tool for achieving goals. You can deliberately program the reticular activating system by choosing your exact messages, goals, affirmations, or visualizations. If you keep thinking that you can achieve your goal, your subconscious will help you to achieve it.

It is important also to understand that your reticular activating system cannot distinguish between real events and 'synthetic' reality. In other words, it tends to believe whatever message you give it. What you can then do is to create a very specific picture of your desired outcome in your conscious mind. The RAS will then pass this on to your subconscious, which will then help you to achieve what you are positively focused on. It does this by bringing to your attention all the relevant information, which otherwise might have remained as background noise.

Something else to consider is the little voice inside your head, the one that chatters away to you all day long telling you all the things that you can and can't do, what you like, what you don't like. We feed our RAS with thoughts and internal self-talk.

Remember you control your RAS – it doesn't control you – so the more attention you pay to what you are feeding it, the more chance you will have to develop that all-important positive attitude and cultivate optimism.

The power of positive intention and how we program our minds can produce much more successful outcomes. The following story sums this up very well.

Once upon a time, there was a general who was leading his army into battle against an enemy ten times the size of his own.

Along the way to the battlefield, the troops stopped by a small temple to pray for victory.

The general held up a coin and told his troops, 'I am going to implore the gods to help us crush our enemy. If this coin lands with the heads on top, we'll win. If it's tails, we'll lose. Our fate is in the hands of the gods. Let's pray wholeheartedly.'

After a short prayer, the general tossed the coin. It landed with the heads on top. The troops were overjoyed and went into the battle with high spirit.

Just as predicted, the smaller army won the battle.

The soldiers were exalted, 'It's good to have the gods on our side! No one can change what they have determined.'

'Really?' The general showed them the coin.

Both sides of it were heads.

LEARNING OPPORTUNITIES

Making mistakes is human and need not turn us into fatalistic pessimists. If we got it right all the time, how would we learn? To increase your rate of success, you will have to be willing to accept that you will make mistakes along the way; the skill is that you learn positively from them. Certainly, some of the best learning and character-building experiences I have been through were on the back of mistakes.

Recognizing and admitting that you made a mistake and addressing what you can to improve the situation can be very liberating.

For example, admitting when we get something wrong and saying 'I'm sorry' can relieve a great deal of tension in any relationship. Humble pie can actually taste quite nice! It isn't poisonous. It is a real skill to be brave enough to admit when you don't get something right and have the humility to accept it, admit it and then positively move on.

Excuse me!

You can create your own self limitations if you focus on all the reasons why you can't do something. If you search hard enough you will find loads of excuses, I am sure. It is really important that you challenge this way of thinking because you will totally limit your potential. You will miss out on so many possibilities and exciting opportunities. Sometimes we make excuses because we are afraid of failing or we fear the unknown, or maybe it is because we are too lazy to give it a go! Challenge yourself next time you make an excuse and really examine the reason behind it!

So granted, life can be an interesting and challenging journey and you may well be faced with some pretty challenging situations and a few painful potholes along the way. Being optimistic takes practice and, certainly, there will be days when you may really struggle to see the bright side. *Desiderata – A Creed for Life* which you will find at the back of the book is a wonderful passage to read, and the following words are a superb mantra to cultivate optimism.

And whatever your labours and aspirations, in the noisy confusion of life, keep peace in your soul.

With all its sham, drudgery, and broken dreams, it is still a beautiful world.

Be cheerful. Strive to be happy.

Positive Steps

1 Make a conscious decision to be an optimist
2 Take personal responsibility and avoid adopting a victim mentality
3 Listen to your self-talk and the internal vocabulary you use
4 Challenge every excuse you make to yourself
5 Embrace mistakes and see them as learning opportunities

See the glass half full – Personal exercise

- Take a small notebook and draw a line down the middle of each page.
- Every time you encounter a problem or negative thinking patterns write them down on the left hand side of the page.
- Once you have written down the negative, flip it on its head. On the right side of the page, write down what you would like the *best* possible outcome to be and then positively focus on that.
- This is an excellent exercise to do before you go to sleep.

Become a possibilitarian. No matter how dark things seem to be or actually are, raise your sights and see possibilities – always see them, for they're always there.

Norman Vincent Peale

TAKE EMOTIONAL CONTROL

*Your emotions are the slaves to your thoughts,
and you are the slave to your emotions.*

Elizabeth Gilbert

*O*ne evening an old Cherokee Indian explained to his grandson about a battle that goes on inside people.

He told him that the battle is between two wolves that are inside us all.

One is called 'Evil' and is full of anger, envy, jealousy, sorrow, regret, greed, arrogance, self-pity, guilt, resentment, inferiority, lies, false pride, superiority, and ego.

The other is called 'Good' and is full of joy, peace, love, hope, serenity, humility, kindness, benevolence, empathy, generosity, truth, compassion and faith.

The grandson listened intently and then, after a while, having pondered the story, he asked his grandfather: 'So which wolf wins in the end?'

The old Cherokee simply replied, 'The one you decide to feed.'

I love this story and it is sums up rather well the control that we can have over our emotions. The crucial question is 'Which are you feeding today?'

EMOTIONAL RESILIENCE

Emotions play a huge part in resilience, and emotional resilience is about your ability to adapt to setbacks and stressful situations by managing your emotions in a positive and helpful way. Understanding the way that you respond emotionally to upset, and learning to regulate and develop an internal locus of control, will be very useful. Emotional resilience is not necessarily a quality that you do or do not possess, there will be varying degrees of how well a person is able to handle adversity. Different people will express themselves in different ways on an emotional level.

A more extrovert person may express themselves in a way that others may perceive as highly emotional by crying or getting visibly upset. Introverts may be less expressive and become quieter when faced with adversity and appear to shut down and hide away. We are all unique and we all deal with our emotions differently, there is no perfect expression of emotion. The key is to ensure that your emotional response is as helpful as it can be and doesn't harm you or others and produce a detrimental outcome. You also need to take responsibility for the way that your emotions can affect others. By being more emotionally aware, you can help yourself to take more self-control and be more resilient in difficult situations.

According to a study at the University of North Carolina, psychologists' research has shown that people who seed their life with frequent moments of positive emotions increase their resilience against challenges. In the month-long study, 86 participants were asked to submit daily 'emotion reports', rather than answering general questions on their happiness history. Those daily reports helped the psychologists to gather more accurate recollections of feelings and allowed then to capture emotional ups and downs.

The study showed that if happiness is something you want out of life, then focusing daily on the small moments and cultivating positive emotions is a very helpful thing to do. Those small moments allow positive emotions to blossom, and that enables you to become more open and receptive. That openness then helps you build resources that will help you rebound better from adversity and stress, to ward off depression and continue to grow.

The emotional dinner table

Your thinking has a very strong influence over your emotions and, as with the earlier story about the two wolves, you can to some degree influence your emotions by addressing the quality of your thoughts. If you allow yourself to get lost in a catastrophic corridor of negative thinking, the chances are you will spiral into a tunnel of unhappiness. If you make a conscious choice to focus on the positive and helpful thoughts you will feel a lot better.

Imagine you are hosting a dinner party for all your emotions and they are sitting around the table, hungrily waiting to be fed. It is up to you who you choose to feed. You can starve the negative emotions and feed up and boost the health of the positive ones with positive thoughts. You are, in fact, the nutritionist of your soul.

Understanding emotions

There are over 600 words in English to describe them and we apparently use over 40 muscles in our faces to express them. Philosophers and psychologists have long debated the nature of emotions, exploring the concept and pondering whether they are cognitive judgements or perceptions of physiological change.

Emotions are an important part of being human, and they help us to protect what's important to us. The way we are brought up, and our culture, will also influence the way we feel. Emotions help us to form ideas and decide what we care about. From an early age we build up our emotional understanding based on the relationships we have with other people.

Emotions can be very powerful and can create some extreme outcomes, especially when anger, passion and jealousy are provoked.

Crimes of passion, and some of the more extreme stories reported in the media, are linked to high emotional outcomes. Our hormones can also influence our emotions, particularly at times of major physical changes in life, such as puberty, pregnancy and menopause.

Jayne was kind enough to share her story with me, one that emphasizes just how powerful emotions can be.

About four years ago Jayne was arrested. She wasn't given a prison sentence but, in many ways, she was very fortunate that her situation didn't escalate out of proportion and she received a series of counselling sessions instead. This is what happened.

Jayne and Simon had been together since they were at college and had moved to the Midlands for his work as a scientist. Jayne had decided to set herself up as a freelance wedding planner and her business had soon taken off and she was travelling all over the country. They had a great lifestyle and decided to put off having children for a while. Then, in her mid-thirties, they decided it was time to try. Jayne, however, experienced three miscarriages before being told that, due to an ovarian condition, it was highly unlikely that she would carry a child to full term.

Both Simon and Jayne were devastated and, despite expensive tests and treatments, the possibility of having a child became less and less likely. Jayne suffered severe depression and became obsessed with having a child of her own.

They were both from large families, with brothers and sisters who had lots of children. At every family occasion, Jayne would find herself in tears hiding in the bathroom and barely holding it together. The strain on the marriage became enormous and Jayne lost all sense of self-esteem, feeling that she was worthless as a woman.

One day it all came to a head when she was shopping in town and decided to stop for a coffee. A young mother with three children was sitting next to her in Starbucks with an adorable baby in a pram. As Jayne sat looking enviously at the family, one of the children tipped his milkshake into the mother's lap. The mother asked Jayne if she could watch the baby whilst she went to the bathroom.

Jayne agreed and, as the mother disappeared, she was consumed by an overwhelming emotional urge. She says, to this day, the memory of the emotion is still immensely powerful. She literally picked the baby up, wrapped it in its blanket, grabbed her bag and left the coffee shop, taking the baby to the park across the road. She found a bench and sat down, rocking the baby and feeling suddenly relieved. Then, literally within minutes, she realized what she had done and ran back to the coffee shop to return the baby. The police, who had already been alerted, arrived and arrested her. However, the mother decided not to press charges and was compassionate to Jayne's story.

Learning to understand your emotions and, indeed, your emotional responses can be very important especially with regard to the way stress manifests itself. One key emotion that stress can trigger is anger, and the term anger management in the workplace seems more common place these days. I have been called in on several occasions to a work environment to work with teams where managers are lacking in emotional resilience.

A few years ago, I was working on a very challenging project around redundancy in a public sector organization. The team I was involved with were very stressed. There was a huge amount of uncertainty and also a distinct lack of information from the top, which created communication issues. Tempers were frayed on a regular basis.

One senior manager who I worked with seemed to be very lacking in 'emotional awareness'. He vacillated – from being passive aggressive, saying very little with the occasional sarcastic remark, creating anxiety everywhere he went – to just 'losing it' and shouting at people, causing staff to get very upset. He would get even angrier when some of the women cried, and his reaction and comments about his female staff was far from PC to say the least. He really couldn't see that his emotional responses were probably causing more upset than all the uncertainty and pressure his staff were under. When I spoke to him and fed back what was happening, initially he really couldn't see the effect he was having. The pressure of the situation had almost blinded him to his own emotions and the importance of taking more emotional responsibility.

DEFINING KEY EMOTIONS

Being emotionally healthy doesn't mean that you feel happy all the time. Positive emotional health is about experiencing a range of different emotions and being able to understand, accept and manage them.

Why do we need emotions?

The range of emotions that we experience will colour our lives and give us depth and differentiation. Emotions serve several physical and psychological purposes, and some scientists believe that emotions are one of the fundamental traits associated with being human. For some people, strong emotions are linked to creativity and expression. Great artists, musicians and writers thrive on arousing emotions to create a connection with their audience. Some scientists also believe that emotions serve as motivation to behave in specific ways.

Emotions also help you to monitor your social behaviour and regulate and control your interactions with others, which is a very useful skill to develop. In the 1990s, Daniel Goleman, who was a scientific reporter for the *New York Times*, chanced upon an article in a small academic journal by two psychologists, John Mayer and Peter Salovey. Mayer and Salovey offered the first formulation of a concept they called 'emotional intelligence'. He later wrote an international bestseller called *Emotional Intelligence* which is well worth a read; and this is now a term that is commonly used, especially in the workplace.

So what exactly is emotional intelligence?

The term 'Emotional Intelligence' was first used in the world of psychology in 1966. The earliest roots of emotional intelligence can be traced to Charles Darwin's work on the importance of emotional expression for survival. Emotional intelligence is essentially the ability to identify, understand and control your emotions and recognize how they can affect others around you. Emotional intelligence also involves your perception of others and understanding how they feel.

Here is a framework that describes five key elements of emotional intelligence:

1. **Self-awareness.** Highly emotionally intelligent people are very self-aware, and self-awareness is something we have

already covered in the first chapter of this book. They are individuals who understand their emotions and, because of this, they don't let their feelings overwhelm them. They also have higher levels of self-confidence because they trust their intuition and don't let their emotions get out of control. They are willing to take a good hard look in the metaphorical mirror so that they can fully understand their strengths and weaknesses and seek to make self-improvement.

2. **Self-regulation.** This is the ability to control emotions and impulses and, for highly emotional people, this can be challenging. People who self-regulate typically don't allow themselves to become too angry or too jealous and they don't make impulsive, careless decisions. Characteristics of self-regulation are thinking things through without being too rash, thoughtfulness, being comfortable with change and demonstrating the ability to be assertive.

3. **Motivation.** People with a high degree of emotional intelligence are also usually self-motivated with a zest for life. They are willing to defer immediate results for long-term success and will put the necessary investment into everything they do. They are generally highly productive, enjoy challenges and are very effective and successful in whatever they do.

4. **Empathy.** Empathy is about having some understanding of, and identification with, how another person is feeling. The metaphor of 'being able to put yourself in someone else's shoes' is often used to describe this. People with empathy are good at recognizing the feelings of others and, as a result, empathetic people are usually excellent at managing relationships, listening and relating to others. Empathetic people avoid stereotyping and judging too quickly, and they live their lives in a very open and honest way.

5. **Social skills.** The final sign of high emotional intelligence is the ability to interact comfortably with others. People with strong social skills are typically team players. Rather than focus on their own success first, they help others to develop and grow. Emotionally intelligent people are good at managing disputes, are excellent communicators and very successful at building and maintaining positive relationships.

So when you read through the key elements and the list of traits it is all very positive behaviour and certainly all those traits will help you to be more resilient. There are many benefits to cultivating emotional intelligence and it is something that can help you in so many areas of your life.

The benefits of cultivating emotional intelligence

Improved resilience

Emotional intelligence will help you to understand and regulate your emotions, which will help you to respond to stressful situations in a much more positive way. By understanding how you are capable of reacting you can create personal strategies that will help you to control your negative emotions in a way that is more helpful for you and those around you.

Improved performance at work

Emotional intelligence can help you navigate the social complexities of the workplace and help you to excel in your career. In fact, when it comes to assessing candidates for a role, many organizations now view emotional intelligence as being as important as technical ability, hence the term competency-based interviews.

Some of the work that I do with the United Nations is based around this. Ensuring that people have the right kind of attitude is key to an organization's success.

Improved physical health

When you are unable to manage your stress levels, it can lead to serious health problems, raising blood pressure, suppressing the immune system and increasing the risk of heart attack and strokes. The first step to improving emotional intelligence is to learn how to relieve stress by regulating and controlling emotions so that you don't become overwhelmed.

Improved mental health

Stress can also impact on your mental health, making you vulnerable to anxiety and depression. If you are unable to understand and manage your emotions, you will also be more susceptible to mood swings. You will feel overwhelmed and out of control which can make you react in a way that you regret and also seek unhealthy coping mechanisms that will just compound the issue.

Improved relationships

By better understanding your emotions, and how to control them, you will be able to express how you feel in a more articulate way. You will also, by developing empathy, understand how others feel and why they react the way that they do. This will allow you to communicate more effectively and forge stronger relationships, both at work and in your personal life.

How to manage emotions

Breathing deeply

One of the best ways to calm high emotion is to manage your breathing. Get into a comfortable position and slowly take in deep breaths, breathing in from your abdomen. This will help to still a racing pulse and calm your mind. Check your muscle tension, especially in the shoulders, neck, and jaw. As you relax any tight areas, picture a peaceful scene, focusing your thoughts on positive images.

Exercise

When you get upset or irate, it will invariably increase your stress levels, so exercise and any physical activity will be good for releasing endorphins. These are neurotransmitters produced in the brain that reduce pain and can change a negative mood.

Write it down

I strongly recommend this as an approach and it is an excellent way to manage your emotions. Keep a journal and write down exactly what you are feeling.

Get it off your chest

Whether it is to a friend or professional, you may need to talk out your feelings to learn how to manage them better. Seek out a good counsellor or a support group where you feel free to share your deepest emotions. The worst thing you can do is to isolate yourself and not reach out for help. At the back of the book you will also find some useful websites.

FOOD FOR THOUGHT

I work with many people who are passionate about the link between emotional health and food. Certainly, in times of stress and change, a healthy body will help to promote a healthy mind and promote resilience. I also know, from personal experience of managing bouts of depression, that diet can have a major impact on the way that you feel. It is very interesting to look at the mind/body link with regards to emotions. A nourishing diet reaches far beyond just simply supporting physical health. Mental functioning, your emotional state and general behaviour are all influenced by the quality and variety of the food you eat. For example, complex carbohydrates are a very important part of a healthy diet. Research has shown that anger, fatigue, depression, and tension are much more prominent in low-carbohydrate dieters than those who balance their protein intake with complex carbohydrates. In order for the body to produce serotonin, a feel-good neurotransmitter responsible for curbing the appetite, improving mood and calming stress, complex carbohydrates are required.

The type of carbohydrate consumed is extremely important to avoid a roller-coaster ride of fluctuating moods. Avoiding sugar-laden foods and starchy foods like potatoes, white bread and white flour is important. These foods create can create a vicious, emotional cycle of peaks and troughs by flooding the system with simple refined sugars. The body compensates by releasing insulin, which causes blood sugar levels to plummet. In response, cortisol production goes into full swing, attempting to balance this downward spiral. As cortisol surges, so does depression and this can trigger yet another cycle of craving refined carbohydrates to boost serotonin and mood.

Omega-3 oils can have a very positive impact on emotional health. Studies show that people who are deficient in this fatty acid have higher levels of impulsiveness, pessimism, and depression. Omega-3 can be found in fish such as sardines, salmon, and mackerel, ground flaxseeds, walnuts, and omega-3 enhanced eggs. Deficiency in iron and thiamine adds to emotional instability as well. Insufficient levels of iron are associated with fatigue, lack of attention, and depression. Foods that are iron-rich include egg yolks, dried fruit, beets, beans, and green leafy vegetables.

Sometimes, when we feel low and crave junk food, it is easy to underestimate the power of our diet on our emotions and resilience. When nutrient-rich food is prominent in the diet, positive mental states are strengthened and the ability to cope better is evident.

THE EMOTIONAL ROLLER COASTER

Life, at times, can certainly feel like an emotional roller coaster and, let's face it, there are some people who even relish the ride. The first step to learning how to feed your emotions positively is to be really honest and open with yourself. Too often people trap their true feelings deep inside through fear. The danger with this is that it can lead to damaging addictions and unhealthy coping mechanisms.

Learning to understand and harness your emotions, and using them to the best of your ability, will help you be more in control and you will be able to turn them into fulfilling experiences with positive outcomes. There are many things that you can do to feed your emotions positively, both mentally and physically, which will in turn develop your emotional intelligence and your emotional resilience.

Positive Steps

1 Understand your emotions and how you respond
2 Learn how to regulate and control your emotions
3 Cultivate your emotional intelligence
4 Observe and understand other people's emotions
5 Develop coping mechanism to manage high emotion

Feed your emotions positively – Personal exercise

- Spend five minutes every morning and evening focussing on positive emotions and feeding them with positive thoughts.

I don't want to be at the mercy of my emotions. I want to use them, to enjoy them, and to dominate them.

Oscar Wilde, *The Picture of Dorian Gray*

4

CHANGE FOR
THE BETTER

What the caterpillar calls the end of the world,
the master calls a butterfly.

Richard Bach

The only future thing of which we can be absolutely certain is that there will be some degree of change in all of our lives. Learning how consciously to direct the changes in your life towards something more positive is most definitely a very important part of being resilient.

Before we start to examine change in more detail, and look at the impact that it can have on resilience, I wanted to share the story of Meredith Murray. She tells us her story frankly and inspiringly, and she has chosen to call it 'Butterflies Are Free'.

On June 20, 1995, my life changed forever.

I think of my experience as a metamorphosis, like that of a caterpillar into a butterfly. My cocoon was my coma; my recovery was my meta-morphosis. I cannot do many things I was able to do before my trans-formation. Yet, I am still the same person. And parallel to a butterfly's entity, I have undergone a complete change.

The Egg

I was submerged in an abyss I had created for myself. From ages 13 to 25, I did everything a parent would not want their child to do. The remarkable thing is, somehow, I survived the drugs, the abuse, and the suicide attempts. My self-esteem was so low at this time, I believed I was ugly and worthless. I rationalized that I would be better off dead.

The Caterpillar

I was driving late at night on a two-lane, unlit, desert road. All that was visible was the moon shadows across the desert, as far as the eye could see.

As the road curved, I saw only the headlights of the 16-wheeler coming toward me, in my lane. I quickly veered to the right, but my car went off the road and flipped, end over end, four times and threw me 100 feet into the sagebrush and sand.

I remember nothing. Where did I go? Was I dead? What did I see when I flatlined? These are all questions that remain unanswered in my head. Does a caterpillar remember what it was like to be a larva after it transforms into a butterfly?

The Cocoon

My family often calls to mind the extraordinary feelings of joy they felt when I finally emerged from my week-long comatose slumber, a caterpillar coming out of its cocoon, changing from one life form into another. I was transforming into a new form of myself.

It did not feel like I was really me. I touched my head and part of my hair had been shaved so the doctors could drill a hole into my skull. They implanted a gauge that measured the pressure in my brain. It stayed there for a week. I could hear myself talking, but I did not know where the words were coming from. It was such a strange experience.

I could not sleep at night. When I moved the pain was unbearable. It even hurt when I blinked my eyes.

My body was not working. I am told I could not hold on to anything. When they put something in my hand, it would just drop open. It was not receiving the messages my brain was sending. Or maybe my brain was not sending any messages.

My brain was not retaining information either. People would tell me things and I would forget what they said, or even if they said anything.

I did not know where I was, who called, or who visited. I was very distressed. All day long I cried.

Nevertheless, I do have one memory of this time. July 1, 1995 at 3:15 AM, I woke up, and not remembering where I was or why, I tried to get out of bed. But the nurses had forgotten to put the guard rails up and I fell to the floor, smashing my head on my wheelchair which was parked next to my bed.

I recall seeing flashes of light and silver when my head hit the floor. I remained there for 20 minutes because the nurse had closed my door and no one could hear my cries for help. I was unable to move because the pain from my broken pelvis was so intense.

Finally, I tortuously crawled to the emergency button and pushed it. The nurses found me on the floor. It was an extremely demoralizing experience and a major setback in my recovery.

Emerging from the Chrysalis

At last, one month after flatlining three times, surviving a week-long coma, and persevering through maltreatment at a recovery home, I was transferred to a rehabilitation institute. Here, I received speech, physical, psycho, occupational, and vocational therapies.

Even with all of the help I was now receiving, I became agitated, angry, disappointed, irritable, guilty, and frustrated. Intense psychotherapy helped me cope with these feelings, maintain a sense of self-worth, and ultimately realize and become grateful for my second chance at life.

I still had some residual effects from the accident, but I was now in the proper state of mind to take on my challenges. I was diagnosed with 'post traumatic amnesia' (no memory eight days after the accident), and 'retrograde amnesia' (no memory two to three weeks prior to the accident).

I had problems processing information and problem solving. A big problem I encountered was anomia, when your brain holds your words hostage. My anomia was a very frustrating component of my recovery. My memory was tested on a scale from 1–100. I was in the 18th percentile. Before the accident, I had been tested and evaluated as 'gifted'.

The Butterfly

Over the last two years, I have worked with disabled people in several group homes. I currently work as a 'Neuro Rehabilitation Specialist' for a wonderful community/job retraining company for brain injury survivors. I have also trained my dog to become a 'therapy dog'. We volunteer at hospital and convalescent homes in order to bring happiness to the patients.

My outlook on life has been transformed. I now look for the good, or the lesson, in every situation and try to turn every negative into a positive. I learned that it is not what happens to you that is important, but how you react to that which happens.

I currently live independently, in charge of my own life. I have made peace with the new me. As a matter of fact, I like the new Meredith and my new life better. This experience has caused me to evaluate and determine what is important in my life and to change some of my destructive behaviours.

I have taken a traumatic life occurrence and turned it into a rewarding metamorphosis. I am so thankful and happy that I am alive today. Whenever I see a butterfly soar by, I cannot help but think how much my life resembles these magnificent creatures.

Butterflies are Free story reprinted with permission by Practical Psychology Press from The Resiliency Center website.

Meredith's story is a really wonderful account of how change, no matter how extreme and unsettling, can create positive outcomes and, as one door closes, many more will open bringing with them opportunities.

Like Eleanor's experience with illness (Chapter 2), it can bring about a new perspective and help you to evaluate what is important.

Modern living has propelled us into a rapidly and increasingly changing world where the escalating pace of change is far greater today than it has ever been. Every aspect of our lives seems to be changing, including the way that we work, the way that we communicate, the way that we shop and eat and, for some, the entire way that we live our day-to-day lives.

It is now quite common for people to change jobs several times. There are those who think nothing of relocating, not only within their own country but also internationally, taking along with them their entire families. It is also now quite common for people to be married more than once, and to have more than one family.

Never before have so many people needed to deal with so many life changing decisions, in so many different areas of their lives, on such a consistent and accelerating basis. Indeed, one of the great challenges of our time is the ability to cope with change. As Charles Darwin observed, the ability to be adaptable is indeed key to survival!

At times, the changes may be only minor; however, on some occasions, they could have a major impact on our lives. A huge amount of upheaval may well cause anxiety, especially if we don't fully understand why the change is happening. It is important, therefore, to attempt to understand why the change is happening and to focus on the potential benefits that it can bring.

We feel much better about the changes that we know or believe are going to make us better off in some way. It is the changes that we are uncertain of, or believe may be detrimental, that we get most anxious about. It is important to remember that, even in the most adverse situations, there will always be something positive that comes from it; we may just need to dig deep to find out what it is.

On a very positive note, it is helpful to understand that change is a vital criterion for any form of development and, without change, there can be no movement or personal growth and development. Certainly it may well cause upheaval, create uncertainty and ruffle a few feathers; however, it can also open many doors to some wonderful possibilities. Making a conscious decision to be positive and open-minded about change will help you to deal with some of the more negative aspects that it can conjure up.

Whilst it is useful to be positive, we also need to accept that we are human and we will experience a range of emotions during the change process. Everyone reacts differently and some people thrive on change and see it as stimulating and exciting. In fact, they seek out ways in which to change their lives on a regular basis, whether that is through work, relationships, hobbies or even something more dramatic. Some people, however, can become very stressed and agitated and see change as something that totally destabilizes their existence.

Understanding how you react to change is important, and intelligently managing those emotions will help you to stay more in control.

The Grief Cycle Model

Elizabeth Kübler-Ross was a Swiss-American psychiatrist. She wrote a book called *On Death and Dying* which included a cycle of emotional states that is often referred to as the 'grief cycle'. She observed that this emotional cycle can also apply to people affected by *any* change that they perceive with negativity.

The basic model has been developed by many organizations to help examine the emotional roller coaster that people experience when they go through change. Some general key stages include:

- **Shock.** This can be the initial reaction when hearing news that may be perceived as negative or unsettling.
- **Denial.** This is very common when people are trying to avoid the inevitable.
- **Anger.** This can be caused by frustration – and an out-pouring of bottled-up emotion – or not clearly understanding why the change is happening.
- **Bargaining.** This is about looking for a way out or attempting to negotiate an alternative.
- **Depression.** This happens when someone perceives the outcome as a negative one.
- **Acceptance.** This is the final stage when people are ready to accept the change and are ready to move forward.

The quickest and easiest way to identify your inner resistance is to observe your own reactions and behaviours as you are experiencing change. Knowledge of this cycle is useful, and making notes of how you react in certain situations will help you to understand yourself better.

A strong sense of self-awareness will also help you to take personal responsibility and stay more in control. It is up to you how you choose to react to each situation.

Learning how to manage change more effectively will help you to be better equipped and more positive when it happens to you. So, here are a few things to think about:

1. EMBRACE CHANGE

It seldom happens that a man changes his life through his habitual reasoning. No matter how fully he may sense the new plans and aims revealed to him by reason, he continues to plod along in old paths until his life becomes frustrating and unbearable – he finally makes the change only when his usual life can no longer be tolerated.

Leo Tolstoy

Sadly, I think this can be true, and sometimes we procrastinate, putting off the inevitable. The danger is that we are wasting precious time in our lives being unhappy when we could turn it all around by embracing change.

2. BE OPEN-MINDED

Your mind is like a parachute: it works best when it is open. Sometimes we can drag the baggage of the past and superimpose it on to situations without being open-minded and taking a fresh perspective. One thing that I hear a great deal from people who resist change is 'Well we tried that before and it didn't work'. Every situation is different, and just because something didn't work last time it doesn't mean it won't work this time.

3. PREPARE YOUR EMOTIONS

Accept the fact that you may be emotional during the change process. In the face of change you may feel unhappy, fearful, insecure, unsettled, frustrated. On the other side of the table, however, you may feel enthusiastic, elated, delighted and excited. Any of those emotions will have an impact on your energy levels so it is really important to prepare yourself.

4. RELAX AND GO WITH THE FLOW

Sometimes change happens and we have absolutely no control over it whatsoever. When this happens you have to choose how you are going to respond. If you resist change and remain rigid and inflexible it will be a lot more difficult and even painful. Going with the flow sometimes is the best approach. It may help to think of yourself as a boat in a storm. If you turn against the waves they will crush you, if you go with them they will carry you home.

5. BE POSITIVE

Having a positive attitude about change is the right mindset to cultivate. If we go into a change situation believing that it is negative then we are more likely to experience negative outcomes. Whilst it is important to understand some of the risks and pitfalls involved it is also important to focus on positive outcomes.

6. KEEP YOUR POWDER DRY

Some people literally panic when change happens because it totally destabilizes their world. If a major change is occurring, try to keep up as many familiar things as you can as a reminder of how much there is in your life that isn't changing. Stick to your usual routines, see people you normally see, and reassure yourself that not everything has to change just because some things have.

7. GET SUPPORT

You don't need to cope on your own, or keep your feelings to yourself. This can actually be very unhelpful; repressing emotion can cause stress. Talk about it, have a hug, try to see the light-hearted side of the situation and get a bit of reassurance. Being brave doesn't really win you any awards these days and will always mean managing your issues alone. It may mean finding the courage to ask for help; however, a supportive friend can be the very best tonic and also help you to get another perspective.

8. CHALLENGE YOUR PERSPECTIVE

Sometimes the way we view a situation can be very narrow because we are perceiving it through our own filter, and will perhaps benchmark it against our previous experiences. It is important to really examine and look at the situation from all angles. Be careful not to get yourself stuck up a one-way street with your thinking. There is always another angle and another perspective.

9. CHUNK UP CHANGE

If you are dealing with a big change, where possible, try to divide the bigger changes into smaller steps. For instance, a house move, a wedding or a divorce involve several stages. When you feel overwhelmed by the enormity of the change, concentrate on the step you've reached, rather than the bigger picture.

10. MAKE A PLAN

Change can overwhelm us, especially when our minds race and we start to imagine all sorts of things that could happen. We begin to catastrophize and, before we know it, we feel completely out of control. A good way to gain control and settle our minds is to make a plan of what we are going to do. Prepare a contingency. Write it all down so that you can actually see it. Very often it's what we don't know and we can't see that scares us the most, especially those of us with wild and vivid imaginations.

Every change will have some impact and sometimes the issue with change is that it has a cluster effect. One change often seems to be followed by several more, and it can feel as though your whole world is changing – and that can be quite overwhelming. It is important to get your head around that so that you can deal with it in digestible chunks.

During World War II the British government created the slogan 'Keep Calm and Carry On', which has become very popular again recently during challenging times. This seems a very apt personal mantra and, certainly from my observation, people who deal most successfully with change are those who stay calm and carry on positively influencing and adapting to the changes that occur in their lives.

Things do not change; we change

Henry David Thoreau

Positive Steps

1 Understand why the change in your life is happening
2 Actively seek out the opportunities that this will bring
3 Be positive and open-minded
4 Understand your emotions around change
5 Take responsibility for your reactions and choices

Change for the better – Personal exercise

- Identify three things in your life that you would like to change.
- Write down why you would like to make changes.
- Write down the benefits to you of making these changes.
- Identify any obstacles that stand in your way and how you can navigate these.
- Set yourself a three-month target and be clear about what results you can realistically achieve.
- Put the date in your diary and schedule a meeting with yourself to review the outcome.

5

COPE WELL
WITH CONFLICT

Conflict is inevitable, but combat is optional.

Max Lucado

There is a really good story that is told about the Buddha, Gautama (563–483BC), the Indian prince and spiritual leader whose teachings founded Buddhism. This short story illustrates that every one of us has the choice whether or not to take personal offence from another person's behaviour.

It is said that, on an occasion when the Buddha was teaching a group of people, he found himself on the receiving end of a fierce outburst of abuse from a bystander who was, for some reason, very angry.

The Buddha listened patiently while the stranger vented his rage, and then the Buddha said to the group and to the stranger:

'If someone gives a gift to another person, who then chooses to decline it, tell me, who would then own the gift? The giver or the person who refuses to accept the gift?'

'The giver', said the group after a little thought. 'Any fool can see that', added the angry stranger.

'Then it follows, does it not', said the Buddha, 'Whenever a person tries to abuse us, or to unload their anger on us, we can each choose to decline or to accept the abuse; whether to make it ours or not. By our personal response to the abuse from another, we can choose who owns and keeps the bad feelings.'

Sometimes when other people choose to vent their angst and project their frustrations onto you it can be really upsetting. I am currently dealing with someone who feels the need to do this, and I can speak from first-hand experience that it can make you feel very anxious. People who choose to host vexatious behaviours can really get under your skin if you are not careful.

It is important to recognize that this is their issue and not yours and there is no benefit in taking it personally. It also helps to remember that if they were truly happy they wouldn't behave in that way so that will help you to feel some compassion, which can be helpful.

It is also important to remember that not all conflict is negative. Sometimes a confrontational situation, if it is managed positively, can bring around some very valuable results. In fact if we never had any confrontation then progress may never be made!

Discontent is the first necessity of progress.

Thomas A. Edison

WHAT IS CONFLICT?

Conflict is essentially when two or more values, perspectives or opinions are contradictory in nature and haven't been aligned or agreed upon. This could indeed be with yourself, when you are not living according to your own values or when your values and perspectives are challenged or threatened by someone else.

Conflict is inevitable and we tend to respond in two ways: we either face it or we run away from it. Stop and think for a moment about a time when you have been faced with a conflict situation. Does it make you want to run and hide away or do you prefer to address it head on? Some people positively thrive on conflict situations and almost relish the stimulation it provides. For example, a 'driver' personality (see later on in this chapter) may well be in their element, whereas an 'amiable' finds conflict unpleasant and would avoid it at all cost.

What is important to learn, regardless of our initial reaction, is that we must be aware of our natural instincts. Whether we feel like we want to fight or flee when a conflict arises, we can deliberately choose a conflict mode. By consciously choosing a conflict mode we are more likely to contribute productively to solving the problem we are faced with.

Conflict can be really positive because it helps to raise and address problems, and can energize the focus to be on the most appropriate issues with a view to resolution and results. Remember, conflict is not the problem; it is when conflict is poorly personally managed that it becomes a problem. Out-of-control conflict can hamper productivity, demotivate and cause continued conflicts that lead to negative, disruptive and inappropriate behaviour.

Conflict can be a hard thing to face; however, there is value in addressing it. A lot of positive things can come from conflict!

THE BENEFITS OF CONFLICT

Create new ideas

Conflict will help you to find new ways of seeing things. If you pay close attention, you may well start to see someone else's point of view and come up with an entirely new way to view things based on the points that have been raised by the conflict. Paying attention and really listening to others is an important part of benefiting from conflict.

Learn about others

Conflict is a great way to learn more about other people. Whether it is an argument with a significant other or a boardroom full of colleagues, facing conflict is a great way to learn more about others. If you pay attention, you will learn not only about their particular points of view, but also about the way they choose to argue. If you pay close attention, you can pick up a lot of information about others when you actively engage in conflict.

Understanding yourself

Another surprising benefit of conflict is that you can learn a great deal about yourself when you are participating in conflict. You learn not only what you believe about that particular topic, but you also learn more about how you choose to raise points, what pushes your buttons, and what makes you more open to others. If you listen to what you're saying and pay close attention to your body language, you can learn a great deal about yourself and your conflict style.

See different perspectives

Whether or not you agree with those you are in conflict with, engaging in conflict will allow you the opportunity to see different perspectives – if you remain open to listening to others. Though you don't have to agree with everything others say, if you want to benefit from conflict you must keep an open mind and be willing to hear what others have to say. You might not agree with another's perspective, but at least you can see it!

Practice communication

Communication is an essential aspect of living a positive life, and dealing with conflict is one way to practice the way you communicate with others. It is, of course, a lot easier to see something from your own perspective and much more difficult to look at it from another person's, especially when we all have such different personalities, backgrounds, ideas, beliefs and values.

Understanding your communication style is very important. Psychometric tests which, translated from Latin, means *measurement of the mind*, are good at helping you to understand your strengths and limitations and how you react in conflict situations. One model that I personally favour is based on four personality types and social styles.

Personality types

Here is a summary of each of the four types and a brief description. It may be worth trying to work out which describes you best. Whilst we cannot cast people into concrete pigeon holes, and we may demonstrate attributes of each style, it is likely that there will be a dominant style.

1. **Driver.** Independent, decisive and determined. Drivers can also be impatient at times and domineering when things don't go the way they want them to. They may feel the need to take control of the situation, which others may perceive as controlling and overbearing.
2. **Expressive.** Good communicator, expressive and imaginative. Expressives can also talk too much, which others may perceive as a bit 'full on' and overwhelming, especially when the level of detail is more than they require.
3. **Analytical.** Thoughtful, disciplined and thorough. Analyticals can also be perfectionists and, on occasion, get so dragged into the minute detail that they suffer from analy-

sis paralysis. For other people, who don't require a huge level of detail to get on with something, it can make them feel impatient and frustrated.

4. **Amiable.** Supportive, patient and diplomatic. Amiables can also be bullied by others and lack the ability to be assertive. Because they don't want to offend, or upset the status quo, they can be hesitant and sit on the fence with a reluctance to make any decisions.

Being aware that we are all different and that we all have strengths and limitations is very important in terms of being able to communicate positively with others. Just because we have a perspective, it doesn't necessarily mean that it is the best one and everyone, no matter what their personality style, has something valuable to offer.

Whilst our personalities may stay the same, we can consciously choose to change our behaviours and reactions if we want, to accommodate others' differences and bring about positive outcomes. On stressful days, when you are under pressure, there is a tendency to revert to form and that is when some of these diverse personality styles can clash. For example, a dominant driver can get frustrated with the laid-back amiable, or the imaginative expressive may find the exacting scientific detail that the analytical goes into a bit tedious.

The skill here is to be aware of your limitations, and to be mindful about how you react, so that your communication doesn't suffer and you can endeavour to look at things from another perspective.

There is a danger that, if we are not careful, poor communication can lead to negativity, insecurity, back-stabbing and blame. This, in turn, can also affect your stress levels and self-esteem, especially when you don't understand something or feel that you have been misled.

Communication can also have a very positive effect on resolving conflict and, when it works well, can make people feel valued, respected and even loved.

Conflict, of course, is more than a healthy disagreement and, when it gets out of hand, it becomes a situation in which one or both parties perceive a threat, whether or not the threat is real.

Here are a few things to bear in mind:

- Conflicts continue to fester when they are ignored, so burying your head is not really a sensible option.

- We respond to conflicts based on our perceptions of the situation, not necessarily on an objective review of the facts. Our perceptions are influenced by our life experiences, culture, values, and beliefs.

- Conflicts can trigger really powerful emotions. If you are not comfortable with your emotions or able to manage them in times of stress, you will certainly struggle to resolve conflict successfully.

- Remember, conflicts are an opportunity for growth and, when you're able to resolve conflict in a relationship, it can build trust. You can feel secure, knowing you can survive challenges and disagreements and you have a resilient relationship.

COPING WITH CONFLICT

Certainly, some people are better at dealing with conflict than others and I have come to the conclusion that some people even enjoy it! How do you react to conflict? Do you fear it and avoid it at all costs? If your perception of conflict comes from frightening or painful memories from previous unhealthy relationships or your early childhood, you may expect all present-day disagreements to end badly. On that basis it is really important that you challenge your fears. If your early life experiences have left you feeling out of control and powerless, conflict may even be traumatizing for you.

If you view conflict as dangerous, it will become a self-fulfilling prophecy. When you go into a conflict situation already feeling extremely threatened, it is very difficult to deal with the problem at hand in a healthy way. Instead, you are more likely to shut down or blow up in anger. If this is the case for you then I suggest that you seek out support because any conflict situation that you deal with successfully will require you to feel confident.

Conflict triggers strong emotions and can lead to hurt feelings, disappointment, and discomfort. When it is handled in an un-healthy manner, it can cause irreparable rifts, resentments and break-ups. When conflict is resolved in a healthy way, it increases our understanding of one another, builds trust, and will strengthen relationship bonds.

If you are out of touch with your feelings, or so stressed that you can only pay attention to a limited number of emotions, you won't be able to understand your own needs.

Manage your response to conflict

Here are few tips for dealing with your own reaction to conflict:

- Manage stress quickly while remaining alert and calm.
- Control your emotions and behaviour. When you're in control of your emotions, you can communicate your needs without threatening, frightening, or punishing others.
- Pay attention to the feelings being expressed as well as the spoken words of others.
- Be aware, and respectful, of your differences.
- Be aware of the language you use and try not to use inflammatory language to convey your message.

In order to handle conflict situations effectively, you will need to learn and practice three core skills:

1. The ability to reduce quickly any stress that is triggered in the moment.

2. The ability to remain comfortable enough with your emotions to react in a constructive way.

3. The ability to deal with things calmly and not to become over-agitated.

If ever you find yourself in a conflict situation with someone and you are looking to defuse the potential volcano that can erupt, this five-step process that I have designed is a great way to cool down the situation.

The 'Cool Down' model

1. **Listen.** When someone is in a conflict mode they can end up being on 'transmit' due to heightened stress levels. By listening and allowing them to get whatever it is off their chest, they will eventually run out of steam.

2. **Sympathize.** This doesn't mean wallowing in a mutual pity party, this means demonstrating that you are in a supportive mode. Simply 'I am sorry that you feel this way' can immediately defuse a contentious situation.

3. **Empathize.** This is about putting yourself in the other person's shoes and attempting to see the situation from their perspective. There are always three sides to every situation. Your perspective, their perspective, and a joint perspective that you and they may well arrive at together.

4. **Ask questions.** Attempt to find out by asking questions what the root of the problem is and what the desired outcome is.

5. **Agree a course of action.** It is always good to discuss a balanced course of action that is mutually beneficial and will achieve the best possible outcome. It may take some time to work out what it is, however it is important that all sides are in agreement and support the action plan.

The cool down model is a good way to defuse the situation. Being aware of what can cause conflict is important too. It could well be poor communication, or not being informed about changes, or simply not understanding another person's motivation. It is important to understand the reasons for decisions. Disagreement about 'who does what', and stress from trying to deal with inadequate information or resources, can be a real irritation.

Personality clashes are inevitable because we are all different, and it can be frustrating when someone doesn't get our point of view. We can also rub each other up the wrong way and often what we don't like in others is what we actually don't like in ourselves.

In conflict we also need to control our emotions and try to not get angry, aggressive or oversensitive. Anger is often stress in denial, and some angry people take pride in their anger and don't want to change; others fail to appreciate the effect it has on themselves and on others. Without a commitment to change, there's not a lot that can be done, anger management is only possible when an angry person accepts and commits to change.

A big factor in persuading someone of the need to commit to change and manage their anger is to look objectively and sensitively with the other person at the consequences of their anger. Often angry people are in denial and put it down to acceptable mood swings and the frustration at the situation as opposed to the way that they are choosing to handle it.

Helping angry people to understand that their behaviour is destructive and negative is an important first step. Most importantly, recognizing how you handle your own emotions is key.

If you know that you can be hypersensitive in certain situations, and take things personally, you need to remind yourself of this in moments of high emotion. It may be that we are so involved with the turmoil that is going on within ourselves that we can become defensive and take it out on other people.

Being as objective as possible and focusing on the benefits of resolving conflict is far more positive and conducive to happy living. It is important, on occasion, to concede that we may not always be right and vice versa. After all, life is rather too short for unnecessary negative confrontation and so much better when we resolve our differences and move on from them in a positive and constructive way.

An eye for an eye will only make the whole world blind.

Mahatma Gandhi

Positive Steps

1 Understand the benefits of conflict
2 Use the cool-down model to defuse tension
3 Consider the other person's point of view
4 Manage your emotional reaction
5 Seek mutually beneficial outcomes

Coping well with conflict – Personal exercise

● Next time you encounter conflict situations implement the cool-down model.
● Review how well you handled each step of the model.
● Identify what areas you need to work on with regards to conflict situations.

6

EMBRACE
PROBORTUNITIES

*Problems are to the mind what exercise is to the muscles,
they toughen and make strong.*

Norman Vincent Peale

Developing a positive attitude toward problems can really help you to recover more quickly from life's obstacles and improve your resilience. You can learn to respond to problems with enthusiasm and eagerness, rising to the challenge to show your stuff and actually amaze yourself with some of the results you can achieve! It is very much about how you view each situation.

I read something once that suggested that problems are opportunities with thorns on, which I thought was a rather good description. Let's face it, we don't exactly wake up in the morning hoping that we will experience problems. However, it is pretty inevitable that we will from time to time.

How you view problem solving is simply a matter of choice. You can, if you want to, view each problem as a giant rock in the road that is an insurmountable obstacle. Or you can work out ways to navigate your way around it.

I was delighted to find that a new word has been introduced into our vocabulary called *probortunity*. This inclusive word combines the word problem and opportunity to describe something you want to improve and change for the better. When faced with any problem at home or in the workplace, try replacing the word 'problem' with 'opportunity' and, rather than focus on the negatives, actively seek out all the solutions and possibilities. Become a possibilitarian!

PROBLEM SOLVING

Problem solving is an important life skill because it is also a very useful tool to help you tackle immediate challenges or achieve a goal. It is a skill because, once you have learnt it, you can use it repeatedly.

There are a variety of problem-solving processes. However, each process consists of a series of steps, including identifying an issue, searching for options and putting a possible solution into action. It is useful to view problem solving as a cycle because, sometimes, a problem needs several attempts to solve it, or the problem changes.

How to solve problems

Here is a process that I recommend to help you break the problem into easier stages, rather than tackle everything all at once.

1. **Identify the problem and focus on solving one aspect at a time.** Identifying and naming the problem will help you find an appropriate solution. Sometimes you might be unsure about what the problem is and you might just feel general anxiety or be confused about what is getting in the way of your goals. When you know exactly what you are dealing with you will feel more in control and actually less afraid. It is also important to have an understanding of what caused the problem. This will help you to put it into perspective and give it some context.

2. **Define exactly what the problem is in the clearest and most simple terms.** Sometimes, problems can seem huge and you may end up blowing them out of proportion with inflammatory language. This is where it is very useful to distil the issue into its most basic terms.

3. **Conduct a root cause analysis, working out exactly what the source of the problem is.** Understanding where exactly the problem came from will also help you put it into context and, going forward, mitigate the chances of it happening again. So some examination of its source is useful. However, over

analysis may be counterproductive so make sure you get the balance right.

4. **Generate a range of potential solutions and make a short list.** When you are clear about what the problem is, you need to think about it in different ways. Seeing the problem in different ways is likely to help you to find an effective solution. This is where creativity can be really helpful, so that you can explore all options available to you.

5. **Use the goal that you are trying to achieve to help you to select the solution.** From the list of possible solutions, you can sort out those that are most relevant to your situation and those that are realistic and manageable. You can do this by predicting outcomes for possible solutions and being clear about the goal that you are trying to achieve. Your goal will ultimately be used to benchmark the success of your chosen solution.

6. **Prepare a plan of action and implement the solution.** Now it's time to create a plan of action. It is also useful to check with other people what they think of your plan and invite feedback. When you have explored all the consequences, you can use this information to identify the solution which is most relevant and is likely to have the best outcome.

Implementing your solution will be easier because you will have so much more confidence knowing that you have really thought it through.

You can prepare yourself to implement the solution by planning when and how you will do it, and who you will need to communicate with for support and co-operation.

7. **Review, identify lessons learnt and record for future reference.** It is always key to review and work out what went well and what you have learnt so that you can make improvements going forward

   Remember, also, just because you have worked your way through the problem-solving process, it does not mean that that you automatically solve your problem. It is advisable to have an alternative backup plan.

Problem solving is a skill, and applying a process which you can learn and practise will not just improve your ability. It is really important to review how you did and make a record of what worked and what didn't so that you can learn and improve your problem-solving skills.

The more you actively and positively embrace some of the challenges that you will inevitably have to deal with in life, the better equipped and more confident you will become. This will provide you with the opportunity to gather a whole raft of experience that will help you to solve future problems. You will also be able to help other people by sharing some of your experiences.

BE CREATIVE

Creativity is a great way for you to explore a wider range of options and to discover new things. It is a useful tool for solving problems, or for when you need to explore new and innovative ways of doing things. It is also something that you may need to do to in challenging economic times, in order to cut back on some of your overheads and save money.

Creativity is an inborn talent of all human beings, and one that can also be developed. It is our creativity that makes us distinct and sets us apart from other animals in this world. When we face challenges, and we are not able to solve them in a conventional way, we knowingly or unknowingly seek creative solutions. In fact, in many ways, the more creative we are the more successful we can be.

Whatever your profession is, creativity is something that can make you more successful and can also make our work easier and sometimes more exciting. By being open to exploring creative channels you can discover a whole range of options and new doors will open and opportunities will arise.

There are lots of different approaches to creativity. One tip I learnt a long time ago was to carry a small notebook with me, and to keep it by the side of the bed too. Often inspiration may strike in the night and it is really good to capture those little gems!

Another good way to let the creative juices flow is to take a walk outside. Fresh air is a great stimulant, and exercise is a good way to help you to release built-up tension so that your mind becomes more open and your ideas will flow.

Brainstorming (or 'mind showers' as they are sometimes called these days) can be an effective way to generate ideas on a specific topic. This technique is particularly useful when you involve others, and bringing together a group of people with different ideas and perspectives can be very enlightening.

Creative thinking tools

There are many creative thinking tools that can be used. One creative technique that I think is really useful, to get a good well-rounded perspective on a creative idea, is Dr Edward De Bono's thinking hats. This is a very popular method, where a team can take on different roles and adopt different thinking styles. Each role is identified with a coloured symbolic 'thinking hat'. By mentally wearing and switching 'hats', you can easily focus or redirect thoughts and ideas.

Here is a brief overview of the different thinking styles:

- **Yellow Hat.** This thinking style symbolizes brightness and optimism. Under this hat you can explore the positives, and probe for value and benefits.

- **White Hat.** This thinking style calls for information known, or that may be needed. It is about getting the facts.

- **Black Hat.** This thinking style is about judgment and plays the devil's advocate and challenges why something may not work. Its role is to spot the difficulties and dangers and potentially where things might go wrong.

- **Red Hat.** This hat signifies feelings, hunches and intuition. When using this hat you can express emotions and feelings and share fears, likes, dislikes, loves and hates.

- **Green Hat.** This hat focuses on creativity and the possibilities, alternatives, and new ideas. It's an opportunity to express new concepts and new perceptions.

- **Blue Hat.** This hat is used to manage the thinking process. It's the control mechanism that ensures that the thinking style's guidelines are observed.

Although this works very well with a group of people, you can also use it on your own by taking an idea that you have and analyzing it from each perspective. For example, if you are the eternal sunny optimist, sometimes wearing the darker pessimistic hat can help to give you a more balanced view.

Creativity can be a huge amount of fun, especially when you use methods like this. It can help you to explore things that you most likely have never experienced before.

It can, at times, take you out of your comfort zone and challenge you. However, it is also very good for you to use creative thinking to keep your brain fresh, stimulated and alert – so there are lots of benefits to this approach.

For some people, taking risks can be quite difficult, especially for those who like to stay well within their comfort zone, and they may well see creativity as change for change's sake. On some occasions, they could well be right; however, until you are prepared to take some calculated risks, you will never know if there is a better or more efficient way of doing something.

We live in a very fast-paced world and, sometimes, we don't allow ourselves time to think. Giving a lot of free time for your mind is an excellent approach. Putting some of your worries and tensions aside for some time every day is very important.

When we are relaxing, the mind is actually working and putting together things that we were thinking of throughout the whole day. It will come out with creative solutions only if we give it enough time and rest. Constantly pondering over endless problems keeps our minds occupied and prevents creativity. So managing your stress levels and de-cluttering your mind is key.

Getting stuck in one way of thinking and trying repeatedly the same methods is a common phenomenon among us. It is also the best way to go a little bit mad! If you have been churning something over and over in your mind and can't seem to find a solution, attempt to stop thinking about it, relax and get engaged in something else for a while. You may well find that when you attend to the problem after some time, your mind views the problem in a different way and a solution may come along straight away!

MAKE DECISIONS

Part of the pain of problem solving can be when we are put on the spot and have to make decisions. Very often there is uncertainty – where many facts may not be known – and you may have to consider many interrelated factors. There are decisions, too, that have high-risk consequences, and the impact of the decision might have important implications for you or for others.

Every given situation has its own set of uncertainties and consequences, and anything that involves interpersonal issues can often be challenging as it is difficult to predict how other people could respond.

All in all, decision making can be quite stressful, so the best way to make a complex decision is to use an effective process. A systematic approach will also lead you to consistent, high-quality results, and can improve the quality of almost everything you do. A logical and systematic decision-making process will help you to address the critical elements that result in a good decision. By taking an organized approach, you're less likely to miss important facts and you can build on the approach to make your decisions better in the future too.

How to make decisions

Here is a critical path that you can take when assessing each situation when you need to make a decision about something:

1. **Identify your decision and establish your objective.** If you have to involve other people it is important to involve the right people and allow other opinions to be heard. It is also important when you make any decision to be aware also of the impact that it will have on others. Whilst you may be prepared to take a gamble, if you are putting others in a difficult position it is important to take that into consideration and act with integrity. Make sure that you are asking the right questions and challenge yourself.

2. **List the various options that you have available.** Being creative will help you to begin the exploration process of what options you have available to you. The more options you consider, the more comprehensive your final decision will be.

3. **Gather as much information as you need on all of them.** When you generate alternatives, you force yourself to dig deeper, and look at the problem from different angles. If you use the mindset of 'there must be other solutions out there', you are much more likely to make the best decision possible and not miss anything.

4. **Conduct a risk analysis and weigh up the pros and cons of each.** When you're satisfied that you have a good selection of realistic alternatives, then you'll need to evaluate the feasibility, risks and implications of each choice.

   In decision making, there's usually some degree of uncertainty, which inevitably leads to risk. By evaluating the risk involved, with various options, you can determine whether the risk is manageable. Risk analysis helps you look at risks objectively. It uses a structured approach for assessing threats, and for evaluating the probability of events occurring.

There will always be some element of risk attached to everything we do as we cannot predict the outcome. Sometimes, we will make decisions that we may well look back on and feel that perhaps another approach may have been better. That is life! We cannot expect to get it right all the time. Also, if we did, how would we learn? If we get caught in a paralyzing loop of fear because we don't want to make a mistake or take a risk, the chances are we would never get anywhere. Sometimes you just need to take a leap of faith.

So, once you have evaluated the alternatives, the next step is to choose between them. With all of the effort and hard work that goes into evaluating alternatives and deciding the best way forward, it's easy to forget to 'sense check' your decisions. This is where you look at the decision you're about to make dispassionately, to make sure that your process has been thorough, and to ensure that common errors haven't crept into the decision-making process.

5. **Select the best option and develop a plan of action.** Once you've made your decision, it's important to develop a plan. You will also need to explain your plan to those who may be affected by it, and involved in implementing it. The more information you can give to people about why you made a certain decision, the better. One of the key benefits of taking the systematic approach to decision making is that you will be able to analyze and evaluate your decision-making process which will, in turn, make it easier to communicate. If you need the support of others, they will also feel more reassured that you have given consideration to your actions. This will be so helpful to you and

to those around you and very much appreciated. As with any change, the more information you provide, the better.

This will also give you personal reassurance that you have thought something through without making a knee-jerk decision.

6. **Implement your decision and stick with it.** Once you have made your decision, stick with it, accept that you have made the best decision based on all the information that you had at the time. Deliberation or indecision will hamper your progress, so go for it and trust in a positive outcome.

   Yes, of course there may well be occasions where you have to accept that you could have done it differently or even better. Give yourself the best possible chance with the best possible information and at least you will know that you did something with your best possible intention and effort!

Problems really can be seen as opportunities, which could well provide you with a chance to get out of a rut you have been in for a while, or a chance to make a situation better. By embracing these probortunities it will help you to seek out innovative ways to deal with each one and you just never know what the rewards will be as a result.

If you only have a hammer, you tend to see
every problem as a nail.

Abraham Maslow

Positive Steps

1 Be positive and view your problems as opportunities
2 Specifically identify and understand each problem
3 Be creative and explore a range of options
4 Determine your goal to help you select your solution
5 Learn to be better at making decisions so that you can move forward

Embracing probortunities – Personal exercise

- Identify a probortunity that you are currently dealing with.
- Define exactly what the probortunity is in the clearest and most simple terms.
- Conduct a root-cause analysis working out exactly what the source of the probortunity is.
- Generate a range of potential solutions and make a shortlist.
- Use the goal that you are trying to achieve to help you to select the best solution.
- Prepare a plan of action of what you are going to do.
- After you have implemented the solution, review the benefits.

LOOK AFTER YOURSELF

The best six doctors anywhere

And no one can deny it

Are sunshine, water, rest, and air

Exercise and diet.

Nursery rhyme

To really master the art of resilience it is very important to look after yourself. A healthy mind will be so much stronger if it is inside a healthy body, so making sure that you invest in your physical well-being is essential.

The real skill in managing your health and daily energy is to work on the more difficult things when you are alert and focused and to work on the easier things when you're feeling lower in energy. One good tip is to get up and get going in the morning. The brain, as a goal-seeking mechanism, likes to get going once we are awake.

Regular exercise will improve mental and emotional health. The chemicals and hormones that are released in the brain through exercise can help deal with stress, promote well-being and provide us with more sustainable energy. If you are challenged with depression, research has shown that thirty minutes of exercise a day can be as effective as a mild anti- depressant. So get up and get going.

Get Active

- **Go for a walk each morning and each evening.** Even if it's just for 15 minutes before and after work.
- **Take the stairs.** Climbing stairs is actually a great workout especially for your legs and bottom.
- **Give someone a massage.** This is one of the best ways to work with your hands.
- **Ride your bike to work.** If it's not too far away this is a great way to get some extra exercise.
- **Go swimming.** Swimming is just about one of the best ways to exercise and it is a great aerobic workout no matter what your physical shape is.

- **Stretch each day.** Stretching helps to prevent muscle cramps and alleviates back pain as well as reducing stress.
- **Volunteer.** Whether it's distributing food to the needy, helping elderly people, or participating in a fundraiser for a worthy cause in your community.

Learning to relax and let go of worry and stress at the end of the day is key. Keeping a clear conscience so that you can relax in the knowledge that you have stuck to your values and principles is one way of being able to clear your mind of anxiety.

Healthy eating with plenty of vegetables and fruit and being light on the fats and sugars is important, as is making sure you are hydrated by drinking sufficient water. Breakfast is the most important meal of the day as it sets you up after a good night's sleep. A good, slow, carbohydrate-releasing breakfast like porridge is excellent for sustaining energy levels. Sugar-rich food will give you a quick energy fix but will leave you feeling even more tired later on. Keeping raw vegetables and fresh fruit as energy-boosting snacks is a far better habit to get into.

It is really important to reduce caffeine and alcohol. Two cups of coffee a day is sufficient, any more and it will affect your energy levels and is not recommended for good health.

Alcohol needs to be within the government guidelines, which suggest 14 units a week for women and 21 for men. It is worth being aware that a large glass of wine can be 3 units!

One of the very best things you can do is to drink lots of water which will keep your body hydrated, flushing out toxins and controlling your appetite. Drinking two litres of water throughout the day is one of the healthiest habits that you can have and I highly recommend this for energetic and healthy living.

POSITIVELY MANAGING STRESS

I think it would be fair to say that a little bit of pressure can be positive. It can, if it is managed successfully, galvanize and help you to perform better at something. However, too much pressure or prolonged pressure can lead to stress, which is unhealthy for the mind and body. Everyone reacts differently to stress, and some people may have a higher threshold than others. Too much stress can often lead to physical, mental and emotional problems.

Stress is your body's way of responding to any kind of demand or pressure. It can be caused by both positive and negative experiences. When faced with a situation that makes you stressed, your body releases chemicals, including cortisol, adrenaline and noradrenalin.

These chemicals give people more energy and strength, which can be a good thing if their stress is caused by physical danger. This, however, can also be a bad thing, if their stress is in response to something emotional and there is no outlet for this extra energy and strength.

Many different things can cause stress. Identifying what may be causing it is the first step in learning how to cope. Some of the most common sources of stress are:

Survival Stress. You may have heard the phrase 'fight or flight'; this is a common response to danger in all people and animals. When you are afraid that someone or something may be trying to hurt you, your body naturally responds with a burst of energy so that you will be better able to survive the dangerous situation (fight) or escape it altogether (flight).

Internal stress. Have you ever worried about things that have happened that you can do nothing about and that you have absolutely no control over? We all do, I am sure, from time to time. This is internal stress and it is one of the most important kinds of stress to understand and manage. Internal stress is when people make themselves stressed and anxious.

Stress releases certain chemicals into your system that can be highly addictive and some people become 'stress junkies' by getting off on a chemical high. They may even look for stressful situations and feel stressed about things that aren't stressful. This, for some people, like coffee, is a stimulant that acts as false energy and motivation.

Environmental stress. This is a response to things around you that cause stress, such as noise, crowding and pressure from work or family. Identifying these environmental stresses and learning to avoid them or deal with them will help lower your stress level. Certainly some people are more sensitive to this than others and find it more difficult to filter out environmental distractions.

Workplace stress. This kind of stress builds up over a long time and can take a hard toll on your body. It can be caused by working too much or too hard and not getting your work-home balance into a healthy perspective. It can also be caused by not knowing how to manage your time well, or not knowing how to take time out for rest and relaxation. This can be one of the hardest kinds of stress to avoid because many people feel this is out of their control.

Stress can affect both your body and your mind. People under large amounts of stress can become tired, sick and unable to concentrate or think clearly. Sometimes, stress can even trigger severe depression and mental breakdowns.

MANAGING STRESS

Here are a few suggestions of things that you can do to cope with stress:

Control your thoughts. One of the best ways to tackle stress is to address your thinking. When the subconscious mind is told something by the conscious mind it doesn't distinguish between what is real and what is artificial. It will believe whatever you tell it. Therefore, if you tell yourself that you are stressed, then you will be. The danger is sometimes stress can become a habit and you may attach a way of thinking to a certain set of circumstances. For example, if you were stressed in a certain situation last time, you talk yourself into believing that you will be again so then it becomes a self-fulfilling prophecy.

Be more assertive. Assertiveness is a great communication skill to develop, especially when we simply do not have enough time on our hands and we have to say no to a request. Also, if you are a passive or aggressive communicator, poor communication skills can add to your stress levels.

Manage your time. A great deal of stress is associated with the perceived time restraints that we have. The feeling that we simply don't have enough time to do everything we need to do is common for many people. We are just about to cover time management in the next chapter so you will learn more about how to do this.

Avoid caffeine. Research has indicated that caffeine increases the secretion of stress hormones like adrenaline, so if you are already secreting higher stress hormones, caffeine will boost it even higher and exacerbate stress/anxiety or depression even further than it already is. By cutting caffeine you will lower your stress hormone levels and therefore reduce stress, anxiety and depression.

Exercise more. The benefits of exercise are numerous, as I hope I have already expressed in the previous chapter. Not only does it release a chemical called serotonin, which makes you feel happier and less stressed, it also improves circulation and helps prevent conditions such as stroke and heart attack. Exercise also allows you to take out your frustration and anger in a constructive way through a very positive channel.

Learn to let go. Learning to let go of the past or things that you fear may happen in the future is a big help when managing stress. We cannot change the past and we cannot control the future. What we can do is deal with the here and now, slow down and go with the flow.

RELAXATION

Building relaxation time into your life is so important. It can help to keep your stress levels down, and consequently maintain and improve your health. Too much work and not enough time out for yourself can result in physical and mental health problems. Taking at least twenty minutes a day to wind down can be enough. Whether it's soaking in a lovely warm bubble bath, or doing a quick relaxation session before going to sleep, or simply listening to some relaxing music.

There are so many wonderful ways that you can relax. Relaxation is the key when it comes to stress relief therapies. Studies have shown evidence of many other benefits coming from regular relaxation treatments. These may include a decrease in the risk of heart attack, protection from mental health issues, a boost for your immune system and even an improvement for your memory.

Stress levels are so much higher than they used to be and it is important for your health to bring these levels down. Finding time for yourself may be difficult; however, it is essential for your well-being that you keep anxiety at bay. If your levels of stress hormones are raised they can cause your blood pressure to rise, making your brain behave differently.

If you are challenged with sleepless nights you will know how it feels to have your mind buzzing with anxiety while you are desperately in need of sleep. Relaxation can help you switch off and promote much better quality of sleep, which in turn will help you to recharge your batteries and cope better generally.

Some people do find it challenging to relax and, very often, I will hear people say that they simply don't have enough time. It can be challenging to find time, especially if you're a generally busy person; however, to avoid burn-out, it is essential to plan in time for relaxation.

One simple method that is easy to build into the fabric of your day is a warm bath. Warm water and a bubble bath will loosen up your muscles and it's a great way to feel pampered without really doing a lot. It will also deepen respiration and take any tension away from your body, which will push all the stresses and strains of the day straight down the plughole! Fifteen minutes soaking in a warm bubble bath will help you feel relaxed and lighten your mind. Candles and calming music can be an additional way to luxuriate.

Music is also a great way of helping you to relax, relieve stress and alleviate any anxieties you may have. It also helps you function mentally and physically, which is why music is a great therapy. It's regularly used for meditation and as an aid for sleep disorders. Studies have suggested that slow, gentle, soothing music can improve learning, creativity and memory.

Relaxation Breathing

Breathing has to be the easiest form of relaxation and, when you focus on breathing, it can really help you to calm down if you are feeling stressed. There are many simple breathing exercises that require no equipment and can be done anywhere.

- Sit with your back straight.
- Place the tip of your tongue behind your upper front teeth.
- Close your mouth and inhale quietly through your nose to a mental count of four.
- Hold your breath for a count of four.
- Exhale completely through your mouth, slowly, to a count of eight.

This is one breath. Now repeat this six times. This simple and effective breathing method will help you to relax.

Another useful relaxation technique is something called 'mindfulness'. The term comes from Eastern spiritual and religious traditions like Zen Buddhism. Mental health professionals are beginning to recognize that mindfulness can have many benefits for people suffering from difficulties such as anxiety and depression. A growing number of scientific studies are showing the benefits of mindfulness in many aspects of our lives including our physical and mental well-being, our relationships and our performance at school and at work.

Mindfulness refers to being completely in touch with and aware of the present moment, as well as taking a non-evaluative and non-judgmental approach to your inner experience. It is essentially about being present and noticing what is around you. So often we can find it hard to relax and be in the moment because we are so preoccupied with the past or worrying about something that hasn't even happened yet.

By focusing on the moment and enjoying the experience rather than being somewhere else, you will heighten your enjoyment of whatever activity you are involved in. Tapping into – and focusing on – all your senses will help you to appreciate much more what is going on around you, which in turn can have a very relaxing effect.

There are also some very good remedies that can work well to help you to unwind. Herbal teas are good, especially chamomile, and lavender drops on your pillow at night can be effective to promote sleep. If you visit your local health store, you can be sure that you will discover a whole host of remedies.

The benefits of building relaxation into your day are multiple and chilling out is a way not only to look after yourself physically, mentally and emotionally, it is also the best way to soothe the soul.

BALANCE YOUR LIFE

One of the big conundrums of modern living is the volume of choices we have available to us and this, in itself, can present us with some challenges. Finding a balance in life, in my opinion, is the ultimate life skill and the one that is the most difficult to master.

Many people spend more time at work than they do at home, and more time with work colleagues than with friends and family; so work is a huge part of their lives. It is now more important than ever that people learn to manage their lives so that they create a better balance and reduce unnecessary stress which, in turn, will promote better long-term health and well-being.

The idea of life balance is further complicated by the fact that today's workforce is more culturally diverse and also made up of different generations, each with its own set of priorities. Additionally, businesses are in various stages of their own life cycles. Instead of looking for a generic, standardized concept of life, we need to understand that it is our own responsibility to make sure that we implement personal strategies that help us to get a clear perspective on how we can better balance our time and energy.

Achieving a Better Balance

Here are a few tips on how you can achieve a better balance.

Create thinking time. Thinking time is very important and, in the fast paced world in which we live, sometimes we don't feel we have time to schedule in thinking. We need to factor this time in, however, and slow down and reflect occasionally; or stop and take stock and amend plans. It is a false perception that you don't have time to stop and think. You need to do this to save time!

Set yourself limits. Setting yourself personal limits is a useful thing to do at work or can be applied to anything else that you tend to do too much of. If you work ten to twelve

(Continued)

hour days, for example, set a limit of eight hours per day and stick to it. Just learn to work smarter and manage your time better and be realistic about what you can achieve in the timescale.

Plan time with family and friends. Plan and literally diarize time for your partner, friends, children or other family members. This may sound a bit regimented; however, it will ensure that you don't end up neglecting those who are most important to you. Be very disciplined about not letting people down. Schedule time with them on a regular basis to do something together.

Develop new interests and hobbies. You are never too old to learn something new and there is just so much out there that you could do. It is really important, with all the demands that you have in your life, that you increase quality time to invest in yourself and your own personal development.

Manage mobile technology. Whilst mobile technology can be very useful it has one of the biggest impacts on our lives simply because it is so intrusive. If you are constantly at the beck and call of your phone then the chances are, even when you think you are spending time with your family, in reality you really are not because you simply are not present with them!

Take holidays. All work and no play. Need I say more? Holidays are the very best way to relax, de-stress and re-charge. It is really important to take the holidays that you are entitled to.

One other important thing to consider is the distinction between work and home, and to be aware of the negativities that potentially we carry between the two. If we are not careful, it can become a bad habit that, at the end of each busy day, we offload onto our partners all the moans and groans of our work day, thus infecting our home lives with the stress of work. A good habit to get into is to spend time at the end of each day sharing your achievements and successes and focusing on the positive outcomes of the day.

Mens sana in corpora sano

This is a famous Latin quotation that commonly translates as 'A sound mind in a healthy body'. Certainly the link between physical and emotional well-being is very strong and, by looking after your physical health in challenging times, it will help you to be able to cope better mentally.

It is very difficult to be strong and resilient when you feel physically tired or sluggish because you haven't been eating properly, taking exercise or relaxing. If you know that you have a challenging period ahead of you this is the time to really invest in your physical well-being. It will also help you to stay focused on doing something very positive. Your health is your wealth, and it needs investment.

A healthy outside starts from the inside

Robert Urich

Positive Steps

1 Refuse the snooze on your alarm
2 Buy a pedometer and walk 10,000 steps a day
3 Reduce caffeine, refined sugar and carbohydrates
4 Reduce alcohol and drink two litres of water a day
5 Build in relaxation and time for yourself every day

Look after yourself – Personal exercise

- Take the 30 day challenge and follow these steps.
- Keep a log of exactly what you eat and the calorific content.
- Buy a pedometer and log how many steps a day you walk.
- After 30 days review the information and make a plan to address healthy changes.

8

MAKE
CONNECTIONS

*It really boils down to this: that all life is interrelated. We are all
caught in an inescapable network of mutuality, tied into a single
garment of destiny. Whatever affects one destiny, affects all
indirectly.*

Martin Luther King

One day a wise woman, who was travelling in the mountains, found a precious stone in a stream. The next day, she met another traveller who was hungry, and the wise woman opened her bag to share her food with him.

The hungry traveller saw the precious stone and asked the woman to give it to him. She did so immediately and without any hesitation, even though she knew how valuable it was. The traveller left, rejoicing in his good fortune. He knew the stone was worth enough to give him security for a lifetime. However, a few days later he came back to return the stone to the wise woman.

'I've been thinking', he said, 'I know how valuable the stone is, but I want to give it back in the hope that you can give me something even more precious.'

'What is that?' the wise woman asked.

'Please can you give me what you have within you that enabled you to give me the stone?'

This is a lovely story about kindness and the importance of making a positive impact on others. In times of loss, adversity and uncertainty it becomes increasingly important to make positive connections with those around you. A strong network of family and friends will help you to feel more supported – we all need a shoulder to lean on from time to time. Cultivating ways to make new connections is really important, especially when you experience change, which itself can create the need to fill a certain void.

There is a danger, sometimes, when we feel low or upset, that we just want to hide ourselves away. However, there is only so long that you can live in isolation, and reaching out for support is really important. Human beings are social creatures and work better when they are interacting with others.

APPRECIATE YOUR FAMILY

I am sure you may have heard the expression that 'you can choose your friends, but you can't choose your family'. However, you can choose the relationship you have with your family. It's easier to take your family for granted than it is your friends, and very often we can be a lot less tolerant and compassionate around our family than we are with our friends. The word family derives from the Latin *familia*, and the old adage that familiarity breeds contempt, sadly, for some families, can be true. Frequently, you hear about upsets and discontent in families and a whole host of long-term feuds and grudges.

There are some very sad stories about family rifts that go on and on for years and years. Some never heal. A while ago, I was doing some work in New York and, on the flight out, I sat next to an American man called Jamie and we chatted during the journey. We talked about the importance of family connections and he told me a very sad story about his family.

Apparently his father and mother had endured a very stormy marriage staying together only for the children and, as soon as they were old enough to fend for themselves, the parents decided to get divorced. His mother had apparently been very bitter and accused the father of having affairs, which he had adamantly denied. Jamie and his sister, who had never had a very strong relationship with their father, took sides and refused to speak to him. The father subsequently moved to London and remarried.

Both Jamie and his sister had children and, despite pleas from his father to reunite, they had both refused. Then his father was diagnosed with bowel cancer and his condition had deteriorated. After a great deal of soul-searching, Jamie decided to contact his father, realizing that he didn't want to lose him without the rift being healed.

He booked a flight with a view to taking his family next time. When he landed, his step mother called to say it was too late. Jamie told me that he had learnt the biggest lesson and that he would actively encourage his children not to bear grudges because you may never get an opportunity to make it right again.

I dare say, we all experience problems with our families from time to time, some more than others. Whether you are living together or apart, you may have family members who you feel interfere or control too much. Perhaps they judge and criticize you. Perhaps there is sibling rivalry and petty jealousies that exist, or lazy relatives who take advantage of other family members.

One thing to consider is that, whatever the situation, they are your one and only family, your gift at birth, so why not make the best of what you have? It really is important to put just as much effort into your family as you do your friends.

The most important first step to learning how to appreciate them more is to stop trying to change them, and work with their strengths rather than focusing on their weaknesses. There are dangers in any kind of relationship if we start trying to change people, rather than celebrating and accepting who they are. No one is perfect – for every strength we possess, we will have an allowable weakness or limitation. It is very unlikely that you will change anyone, so the best approach is to change your own attitude and see the positive in everyone.

Making an extra effort can make all the difference. If you really want harmony in the family, perhaps just taking that first step is all it takes. If two people are stubbornly fighting with each other and one decides not to argue anymore, it leaves room for change. We all have quirks and habits that will annoy and irritate people, but bear in mind that what annoys or irritates us about someone else is very often what we don't really like about ourselves. Tolerance, and a measure of empathy, can carry us a long way towards creating harmonious relationships.

Each person's well-being and happiness can be supported and nurtured by their family. Unfortunately, most people tend to neglect their families, especially when busy pursuing their career or other activities. What some people can forget and overlook in their busy lives is to spend quality time with the people they love. Family is the prime factor that helps most people succeed in their careers. For this reason, it is vital that there should always be a balance between work and family.

Today's competitive world makes work very demanding and stressful. It does not only mean meeting deadlines and handling projects, but the schedule in itself can be very hectic and it is important not to bring stress home. Stress can be eliminated if you spend quality time with your children and loved ones at home. The very fact that you will be surrounded with their laughter and love can already take away the stress that has been with you at work. It simply invigorates your mind and well-being as a whole. Leisure time spent with your family is the perfect time for you to become fresh and energized, which ultimately helps people to work better.

Every quality moment spent with your family encourages better communication. You get to understand them better by learning what they like or need. The time you spend with your family will simply strengthen your relationship and the love you share. For this reason, it is very important that one should balance life at home and at work. Having your family at your side supporting you will give you the strength to surpass all the challenges life brings.

Family matters

Here are a few tips to help you appreciate your family more and develop healthier and happier relationships:

- Spend quality time with your family and be present with them when you are with them.
- Learn to be positive about your family and seek out and celebrate the things that you like about them.
- Learn about them as 'people' and take an interest in what they do, what they know and how they actually feel.
- Respect and try to see their point of view as you would anyone else.
- If you are upset about something, talk about it, don't just bury it under the carpet and hope it will go away – it won't, you will just find yourself sitting on a pile of dust.
- Have a sense of humour and find the funny side of situations so your home environment is light and happy.
- Be careful about bringing your own stress into the home and family environment and take personal responsibility for your emotions.
- Don't have the TV on every night. Play games, make things; talk.
- Ask each other questions and really listen to the answers.
- Try to get out in the evenings and go for a walk altogether.
- If you live apart, get on the phone and make contact regularly.
- Be a friend to every member of your family and help others to do the same.

CULTIVATE AND NURTURE FRIENDSHIPS

According to a study documented in the June 2006 issue of the journal *American Sociological Review*, Americans are thought to have been suffering a loss in the quality and quantity of close friendships since 1985. The study states that 25% of Americans have no close confidants, and the average total number of confidants per citizen has dropped from four to two.

The friendships in my life, along with my family, are the most important thing to me, and every day I appreciate them and am truly thankful for how special those relationships are. There is an expression that says, in order to really understand the soul of a person, look to their friends! My friends listen to me, try to understand me, tell me when I am doing something that may not add value, make me laugh and smile. The trust that has developed within each of these friendships gives me a security and a faith that I would not want to live without.

The popular definition of a friendship is that of a form of interpersonal relationship generally considered to be closer than association, although there is a range of degrees of intimacy in both friendships and associations. True friends, in my perspective, are there for the good times and the bad and love you for all your idiosyncrasies.

Friendship has been a very popular topic of moral philosophy, discussed by Plato, Aristotle, and the Stoics. Aristotle writes that:

*The excellent person is related to his friend in
the same way as he is related to himself, since a
friend is another self; and therefore, just as his own being
is choice-worthy for him, the friend's being is choice-worthy
for him in the same or a similar way.*

Research indicates that people with strong and broad social relationships are more resilient, happier, healthier and live longer. Close relationships with family and friends provide love, meaning, support and increase our feelings of self-worth. Sustaining friendship takes conscious effort. It is important not to take your friendships for granted, and showing appreciation is key.

Making others feel good

When you want to show appreciation to your friends for their friendship, there are a number of things you can do.

- Show gratitude for a great friendship by reciprocating acts of kindness and generosity.
- Tell them and thank them and explain how it made you feel when they do something you appreciate.
- Make mental notes about what you appreciate about each friendship and do the same for them – to have a friend you need to be a friend.
- Tell your friends how much you care about them. Life is too short to miss the opportunity.

RELATIONSHIPS AND RESILIENCE

There will be times when you get let down by people, or perhaps a relationship has become so broken it is beyond repair. This can be very upsetting – break ups and divorce can be incredibly painful.

I remember once reading a passage of writing after a relationship ended called 'Reasons, Seasons and Lifetimes', which suggests that people may enter your life in these three ways. Sometimes it may be for a reason; perhaps to teach you something or to help you in a very specific way. If they enter your life for a season, it may just be for a brief period of time and, just because it hasn't lasted a lifetime, it can still give great pleasure and be a positive experience. Others may well enter your life and be with you throughout.

This concept is a very good way to view relationships because some simply do not last forever and letting go can be a very challenging experience and one that can be tough to bounce back from.

CONNECT TO YOUR PURPOSE

Making connections isn't just about connecting with other people; it can also be about connecting to your purpose and feeling that you are adding value. A great deal of research now suggests that people who have meaning and purpose in their lives are happier, feel more in control and get more out of everything they do. They also experience less stress, less anxiety and are less prone to experience prolonged bouts of depression.

We all need to stop and explore our purpose, rather than racing around like headless chickens wondering what it's all about.

It helps us to answer the burning questions of 'Why are we here?' and 'What's it all about anyway?' Often it's something that can't be distilled into one definitive thing and goes far beyond our day-to-day activities. It guides us in how we choose to live our lives and what we strive for, and provides a framework and measurement for the goals that we set ourselves. It can help us to make sense of what happens to us. It can provide a source of comfort and strength in challenging and difficult periods of our lives and, most of all, helps us feel that we are not alone, because we are part of something much bigger.

We have a purpose to be kind and considerate in our behaviour towards others. By taking more personal responsibility for the consequences of our actions, our purpose becomes more honourable. I like the concept that we are all connected and that if we hurt others, we will only end up hurting ourselves. If we approach every life situation with positive and kind intentions, then we will be making our own great individual contribution to creating a better world.

FINDING MEANING

For some people, finding meaning comes through experiences, often difficult ones. Other people find their meaning through deep reflection, others from loving and being loved and others just from the way they choose to approach other people and the world around. We can each find our own way – but it's important to remember the importance of meaning when making the big choices about our families, jobs, lifestyles and priorities.

Some people see their meaning as finding their 'calling'. What is certain is that 'meaning' is something very personal. No one else can tell us what gives meaning to our lives and, if we rely on others rather than taking personal responsibility, we leave ourselves vulnerable. We have to discover different ways of finding meaning. We need to explore and identify and pursue our own purpose with a positive intention of making the world a better place.

MAKE A DIFFERENCE

Lead the way. A good example has twice the value of good advice. When we endeavour to do things to make a difference, we should also seek to influence others to start doing things that make a difference too. The best way to convince other people is to lead by example. Start doing whatever is within your ability today. Start showing more consideration for the people you live with, work with and come into contact with each day. Every effort counts, no matter how small and insignificant it may seem. Just do something, and do something good.

Respect and value others. I am sure that you have witnessed someone getting treated unfairly. It happens both professionally and socially, sometimes individuals who deserve recognition do not get it. Perhaps they are scared of confrontation and find it hard to stand up for themselves. By taking up the fight and making sure others get what they deserve you will make a lasting impact on their lives. They, in turn, will get the justice they deserve and feel better. Be careful that you get all the information right though before you go jumping in feet first.

Random acts of kindness. There are so many that you can do. It's the little things that can make another person's day, like helping someone with a heavy case or a pram, holding open a door, picking up some litter. It really doesn't need to be huge. Having the courage to compliment someone if they look nice is lovely and can make them glow all day. You have most likely been on the receiving end of some kind act so I am sure you know how good it makes you feel.

Develop an attitude of gratitude. Making a conscious decision to be grateful for who you are and what you have in your life is a very positive way to behave. This will also help you to value everything that you have in your life and not take anything for granted. Research suggests that if you practise gratitude on a daily basis after 28 days you can increase your happiness levels by 25 per cent.

Be happy. Happiness and love are two of the greatest gifts you can give to the world. Too often we are so absorbed in our own little bubble that we forget that there are people in this world who we can make a little happier and who we can make feel a little more loved.

You can make a difference right now to yourself and the world around you and be happier. If you know that you are doing the best you can every day in every way then you will know that you add value, and your purpose in life will be to know that you can make a positive difference in everything that you do.

There are so many ways that you can create positive connections in times of difficulty. Looking upwards and outwards rather than internalizing will help you to see that there is a big wide world out there that you can reach out to, and connect with.

You may say I'm a dreamer, but I'm not the only one. I hope someday you'll join us. And the world will live as one

John Lennon

Positive steps

1 When you feel low, make an effort to connect with people
2 Appreciate and accept your family for who they are
3 Cultivate and nurture your friendships
4 Be open to exploring and making new connections
5 Define your purpose and contribute to your community

Make connections – Personal exercise

- Identify one new interest outside the workplace that you would like to explore.
- Search the internet and do some further research about the interest.
- Join a club or online community that appeals to you depending on the time you have available.

9

KEEP GOING

If you are going through hell, keep going.

Sir Winston Churchill

I love this quote by William Churchill because, let's face it, sometimes when the chips are down, it really does feel as if you are literally going through hell. When you experience so much pain, loss and disappointment it's almost impossible to believe that it can get any better. However, this is the time where you need to tap into every resource you possess and keep going. Another of Churchill's finest observations was that success is not final, failure is not fatal; it is the courage to continue that counts.

I would like to share with you the story of my friend Adam Balding, a professional rugby player who, during his career, has had to deal with many knock-backs. When I first started writing this book, Adam and I had begun to work on a programme called Team Tonic, which is about helping teams to be able to deal with tough times and build more resilience through attitude and determination.

As I listened to Adam's story, it became clear that a truly resilient mindset is about having the ability to see every obstacle as a challenge and to keep a firm belief that things will eventually get better.

Adam has been the Captain of Gloucester Rugby Club and played for Leicester Tigers, Worcester Warriors and Newcastle Falcons as well as winning a variety of cups and competitions.

He joined Worcester Warriors for the Aviva premiership. After a gruelling training period he then played the first game of the season against an Australian team called the Melbourne Revels. Twenty minutes into the game there was a pile-up and he broke his toe in two places. As a result he was told he would have a three-week layoff. Disappointed, he accepted this and was determined to view it as an opportunity to focus on ways he could improve his game. He used visualization techniques and a positive belief that he would get better and be fighting fit again soon.

Just as he recovered, he experienced another setback and injured his back, which led to another three-week layoff. This time, he could do no physical training, so he again focused on visualization and watched videos of games to focus on strategy and improving his techniques. After his recovery he then started to play again and, for seven weeks, his game grew from strength to strength.

Then during a game in Italy he slipped and was tackled at the same time and tore his hamstring tendon off the bone. The devastating news was delivered that he would need a 12–15 week recovery period.

At this point, Adam knew he had to draw a line in the sand and accept his situation. He made a very clear and conscious decision to accept his circumstances recalling his father's advice to focus on 'controlling the controllables'. Adam knew that success was 80% about mental application and 20% about physical so he worked hard psychologically to prepare for recovery.

After eight weeks he was declared fit and given the green light. However, as he got back into training, he sensed that something wasn't right and approached the coaching team to express his concerns. He asked for honest feedback and they honoured this by telling him that, due to his series of freak injuries and despite his recovery, he was not in their plans to move forward in the premiership team.

Adam accepted this, and was totally appreciative of their honesty, because this then provided him with the opportunity to make some choices. He could either stay or go on loan to a different premiership. He was offered the opportunity with Newcastle Falcons who were bottom of the league.

A new coaching team had been put in place and Adam saw this as a great opportunity to experience something else. Adam attributes their success to the amazing coaching team headed by Gary Gold from South Africa who shared personal stories of resilience and was a total advocate of change. Gary's belief was that too much of one thing isn't good for you and change provides challenges that strengthen and motivate.

Adam says he will never forget this experience and the time leading to the final game in the season which they won. Through adversity his appreciation of success is sweeter and his belief is that success is the journey, not the destination.

No matter what happens to you, it is essential to pick up the pieces as quickly as you can and focus on the potential that is out there. Remember that the greatest oak was once a little nut which held its ground!

The ability to keep going through times of adversity is essential because the alternative is one of defeat. One piece of advice that I have been given through some of my darkest times has been to remember that this time will pass and that is the truly amazing thing about life: the excruciating times do ease and, when you keep the faith and really trust that things can and will get better, they do.

LEARN TO LET GO

One of the most powerful behaviours of resilient people is their ability to let go of the past and lose some of the baggage that we invariably collect along the way.

I recall an experience, from a couple of years ago, of a woman I met while I was doing some training on emotional resilience in Vienna. Throughout the course she was spending a great deal of time bringing up the past and getting highly emotional about negative relationships, previous jobs and bosses, and general issues around rejection. Each tale she told she described in micro detail and, each time, in her mind she was visibly reliving every moment of each ordeal. She seemed to have collected and stored away each traumatic experience and wanted to bring them out and air them on a regular basis. The intensity of her emotion around each situation was so tangible it was almost as if she was actually living the experience there and then.

The issue with carrying baggage is that you can end up reliving and rehashing all your nightmares and trapping yourself in a paralyzing loop of negativity. Making a conscious decision to let go and free yourself is key. Many people talk about burying the past – however, the danger here is that, if you bury it, you will just go back and dig it up! Without freedom from the past there really is no freedom to embrace the future.

Letting Go of Your Baggage

- Ask yourself a very fundamental question. How am I benefitting from reliving my negative past? Once you clearly understand that it doesn't serve you in any way it will help you to detach yourself from it. Learn the lesson and move on.
- Paul McGee wrote a fantastic book called *SUMO – Shut Up and Move On*. This is a great bit of advice if you are anything like me and have the propensity to over-analyze. Let's face it: kicking the past around is not only exhausting; it can also be really boring!

(Continued)

- Write a letter to yourself about the negative experience and then destroy it and make a conscious decision to let the experience in your mind go at the same time.
- Start working on new memories. If you focus your mind on the present and start to create dreams for the future, this will help to take your mind off the past.
- Under no circumstances 'should on yourself'. If you hear yourself saying 'should have', 'would have' or 'could have' all you will do is make yourself feel disappointed and regretful. So you didn't – so what? You can now, if you really want to!

No matter how hard the past, you can always begin again.

Buddha

CONTROL THE CONTROLLABLES

If we attempted to control everything in our lives, it would be like trying to clutch the ocean in the palms of your hands. Sometimes we simply need to accept a situation. Some things, however, we can control and we can be brave enough to make changes. You may well be familiar with the Serenity Prayer which is a good mantra for life and would save a huge amount of wasted energy if the wisdom to know the difference can be mastered!

God grant me the serenity

To accept the things I cannot change;

Courage to change the things I can;

And wisdom to know the difference.

Develop healthy coping mechanisms

We will, of course, all react differently to trauma and stress in our lives. Some people take a more stoic approach and keep their feelings hidden; others may become more expressive and emotional. Different personalities tend to process information in a variety of ways and your reaction will be part of your coping mechanism.

You need to be mindful about some of the unhealthy coping mechanisms that can be triggered as a result of grief and pain. I heard an expression once, which is apparently Scottish, and is about 'knowing your beastie'. This refers to the fact that many of us have the propensity to gravitate to a range of bad habits when we are upset or feel out of our depth. I have outlined five of the most common unhealthy coping mechanisms which you may well recognise as your 'beastie'.

Emotional eating. Eating all the wrong things is one of the most popular coping mechanisms for stress and this can lead to compromised health, weight gain and additional stress caused from lack of essential vitamins. Comfort eating is a very quick fix and a moment on the lips can be a lifetime on the hips! It is important to remember that we are what we eat, and if we stuff ourselves with junk food we will feel rubbish. In times of trauma and upset, a diet that fuels your body with premium energy is so important.

Excessive alcohol. Certainly a glass of wine can be a good way to unwind, and most researchers and physicians agree that a very small amount can indeed have some health benefits. However, drinking alcohol when you feel upset can be a very slippery slope. I will openly admit that I have explored the concept of seeking solace at the bottom of a bottle during difficult periods and I can categorically say from personal experience that you won't find it!

Alcohol is a depressant, so the best thing you can do when you feel low is to avoid alcohol altogether, especially if you are incapable of moderating your consumption. Better to enjoy a drink as a treat when you are feeling good about life rather than trying to mask your pain or anxiety.

Compulsive spending. During times of loss and uncertainty the need to fill a void can be quite overwhelming and a quick pick-me-up may seem appealing. Retail therapy can often be referred to in jest; however, this can have a serious impact on your life – especially if you are spending money you don't have. While credit cards can be convenient, they can also get people in a huge amount of trouble and financial stress is becoming an increasing problem. Online gambling, or indeed any form of gambling, can become a huge issue as people look for an instant fix of hope or escapism.

Smoking. For smokers, a cigarette can feel like a good stress reliever. However, contrary to popular belief, smoking does not help to combat stress. In fact, it can make it worse and cause damage to your body. Giving up smoking is not easy and it has been suggested that it can be as difficult as giving up heroin. There are, however, so many support programmes and services available now that can help you to quit and you will be giving yourself the greatest gift of all: the gift of health.

Caffeine. People every day enjoy a daily dose of caffeine and whilst this may seem the most innocent of vices, caffeine can exacerbate or even cause stress, anxiety, depression and insomnia because it interferes with a tranquilizing neurotransmitter chemical in the brain called adenosine. This is the chemical which turns down our anxiety levels; it is our body's version of a tranquilizer. Research has indicated that caffeine increases the secretion of stress hormones like adrenaline. So, if you are already secreting higher stress hormones, caffeine will boost it even higher and exacerbate anxiety or depression even further than it already is. It is best to avoid drinking anything containing caffeine when you are upset. A good alternative, I find, is ginseng herbal tea.

This is, of course, not an exhaustive list and, when I was doing my research, I came across a whole host of vices that made my eyes boggle! Other unhealthy coping mechanisms that can occur include self-harm, illegal drugs, shoplifting, internet porn addiction and a variety of mental health issues.

At the back of this book, I have cited a range of organizations which may be useful in supporting you if you find that you unable to manage some of your unhealthy habits.

Seek out healthy coping mechanisms

Earlier this year, immediately after my father's operation, I had to have a cataract operation on my eyes due to a hereditary ocular disease. Perhaps it was partly due to the hangover of stress from my father's illness or that I am a complete wimp; however, the operation was hugely traumatic for me. The experience of having a needle in my eye ball and my eye scraped and cut (under anaesthetic) was something that I couldn't shake and every time my mind dragged me back to the experience, I felt as if I was going to be physically sick.

I started dreaming about decorative arrangements of needles with multicoloured eyeballs on the end and I found that a lot of things I looked were becoming distorted and representing that image.

So I was feeling sick a lot of the time. This was causing me to feel incredibly emotional and overwhelmed.

I spoke to my friend Cindy about this who had been practising Emotional Freedom Therapy (commonly known as *tapping*). Emotional Freedom Therapy (EFT) is a form of counselling intervention that draws on various theories of alternative medicine including acupuncture, neuro-linguistic programming, energy medicine, and Thought Field Therapy. Tapping on meridian points on the body, derived from acupuncture, can release energy blockages that cause negative emotions.

This was an incredible experience for me and, after one session and lots of practice, I have now managed to overcome the sickness and don't feel traumatized by the memory at all. I have listed some websites at the back of the book and I would highly recommend this as an option to releasing negative baggage.

Reach out for help

To help you to keep going there will be times when you simply need to reach out for help. Some people take 'I can cope!' to an extreme and believe they can do it all by themselves; however, as we have already established, we need to make positive connections and we need other people. Listening to how other people have kept going through pain and adversity can help to trigger ideas in our own minds. There is nothing to be ashamed of in reaching out.

Seeking out a counsellor, a coach or a mentor can be really useful to help you see another perspective. A good coach will help you to find your own answers by self-actualizing through the process. Offloading some of your built-up anxiety and fears will help you to lighten the load.

Be kind to yourself

Isn't it great to know that you are a person in progress? Imagine how boring it would be to be the finished article! Every day will bring new experiences: some may well test you and some may well nourish you and bring with them some lovely surprises. It makes getting up in the morning well worthwhile. An acceptance of your limitations and a celebration of all your strengths and good points is important when you are feeling up against it. It isn't the time to start self-sabotaging and challenging yourself. It is important to be kind and gentle with yourself as you would with any friend who was going through a bad time. So give yourself total permission to give yourself a daily dose of tender loving care.

Take some time out

I think I used to adopt a bit of a gung-ho attitude to stressful times in my life and believe that 'keeping going' was all about 'marching on'. I am beginning to understand, however, that the ability to keep going is also about pacing yourself, especially when life's little conundrums are taking their toll. Slowing down and moving at a pace that you can cope with is very important, not just for your physical well-being, but also mentally and emotionally. Some people have a tendency to start rushing around and over-occupying themselves when they get unhappy. All this does is mask the issue and bury it – and then it will come back and bite you when you least expect it to.

Be inspired

During the last few years, I have been visiting some fairly incredible places as an international consultant with the United Nations.

This has taken me to places like Afghanistan, Cambodia, Ethiopia and Beirut. The people I meet who work for the UN in Duty Stations and Peace missions are really diverse and have so many extraordinary experiences. People who have witnessed atrocity and those who have risked their lives tell me so often that what keeps them going is seeking out inspiration.

This may be about observing the actions of others or exploring more details about great leaders, reading books and taking inspiration from music or poetry or quotations. This can indeed be a powerful tonic and, certainly, the creed for life in the back of the book called *Desiderata* has been a constant inspiration to me. Throughout this book are quotes that people have shared with me along the way. Small sound bites can be a very effective pick-you-up. Music, as well, can be a very evocative tool, especially some classical tracks and also songs with poetic and meaningful lyrics. Do take a look at my top twenty bounce-back songs at the back of the book.

Smile

A few years ago, when I lived in London, I used to spend quite a lot of time watching live comedy. I have a great deal of admiration for people who can stand up on stage and open themselves up to what can be a very challenging audience, and even be subjected to abuse and torment. When I give talks on cruises I get to know lots of the comedians and hear all about how they collect materials. Something that I have found is that many comedians experience depression and a great motivator for them has been to turn some of their darker experiences into comic episodes.

I met Frank on a ship a few years ago. He had been on the comedy circuit for less than five years. However, he had become very popular, very quickly, after a successful debut at the Edinburgh festival along-side various TV appearances. When I heard about Frank's life story I was in awe at how he managed to smile let alone stand up on a stage and tell jokes.

Frank had experienced a succession of tragedies in his life. When he was ten his parents had been killed in a car crash and he had been brought up by an aunt who was a widow and had no children and had seen him as a bit of an obligation that had been thrust upon her. She was very strict about him mourning his parents, so he was forced to suppress emotion which caused him to become aggressive and get into fights at school. He was then put into care and became more disruptive and, later, became involved in crime, which resulted in a two-year prison sentence for theft. When he came out of prison he made a decision to reform and got a job as a landscape gardener. A year later he met his wife Lucy at a comedy club where he was attempting his amateur comedy routine at an open night. Apparently, she thought he was the funniest comedian and came to get his autograph.

He describes Lucy as his soul mate and salvation and she actively encouraged him to develop his routine and pursue a career as a stand-up comedian. He worked hard on his routine and started to make progress and cultivate a reasonable living and then Lucy was diagnosed with breast cancer and, despite various chemotherapy treatments and surgery, sadly died. Frank said he was devastated and seriously considered taking his own life. He knew, however, that Lucy would want him to continue his life in a positive way and in her words 'make the world smile' which is exactly what he does.

It may sound impossible when you are feeling low and despond-ent to see the happy or funny side of anything. Humour, laughter, or simply just turning the corners of your mouth upwards, can have a profound effect and help you to take that next step.

Smiling is the gateway to laughter and smiling. Like laughter, it is also contagious. Start off by smiling at simple things, and make a conscious effort to smile more often. Apart from making you feel good, smiling also makes you more attractive. People are naturally drawn to people who smile easily, and a smile can change your mood and help you to feel positive.

Smiling is also a natural drug and, when you smile, your body releases endorphins and serotonin. Endorphins are also known as the body's natural feel-good chemicals or natural painkillers. Serotonin is a hormone that is found naturally in the human brain. It is known as a 'happy' hormone, because it influences an overall sense of well-being. Serotonin also plays a part in regulating moods, tempering anxiety, and relieving depression – so a whole host of benefits here!

There are so many ways to keep going and, sometimes, it is simply a question of believing that the tough times will pass. Acceptance, change, loss, pain and trauma are part of the rich pattern of life, and something that we all have to endure. Remembering that you are not alone can also help because it is the loneliness of unhappiness or depression that can make you feel so isolated. As my father used to say, 'Here we suffer grief and pain and over the road they suffer the same'.

With that knowledge, when you are feeling loss, seek out others who you can help to support. We are all in it together and, through the roller coaster and crazy playground that we call life, we all have the capability to keep going, upwards and onwards.

I've missed more than 9000 shots in my career. I've lost almost 300 games. 26 times, I've been trusted to take the game

*winning shot and missed. I've failed over and over and over
again in my life. And that is why I succeed*

Michael Jordan

Positive steps

1 Learn to let go of the baggage from your past
2 Explore healthy coping mechanisms
3 Seek out counselling, coaching or mentors
4 Be kind and gentle to yourself
5 Seek out inspiration to keep you going

Keep going – Personal exercise

- Write yourself a letter and list all the things in your past that you would like to let go of.
- If you do it on the computer, double-delete.
- If you write it down on paper tear it into as many pieces as you can and throw away (this is physically very therapeutic).
- Make a conscious decision not to revisit those experiences.

10

CREATE A VISION

*Man is a goal-seeking animal. His life only has meaning
if he is reaching out and striving for his goals.*

Aristotle

Our vision is our guiding light and we all need light especially at times when we feel we are in a long dark tunnel. In many ways it is a survival mechanism.

Various experiments have been conducted with mice which show that when they are placed in a bowl with no way out, they would stop swimming after 45 minutes and drown. However, if the mice had a light shining on them, they would continue to swim for 36 hours. The mice were motivated through the darkness by a vision of light. Certainly hope and optimism are huge factors with regards to resilience. In times of darkness we need to believe that there is something out there that is better and worth waking up for in the morning.

The day that I began writing this chapter was the day that Neil Armstrong died. At 82 he had lived an incredible life as a true national and international hero in the classic sense. His intellect, dedication and skills made him absolutely the best choice to be the first American and first human being to set foot on the moon in 1969 as commander of Apollo 11.

On his greatest achievement he commented:

> *I think we are going to the moon because it is in
> the nature of the human being to face challenges.
> It's by the nature of his deep inner soul – we're required
> to do these things just as salmon swim upstream.*

When Neil Armstrong stepped on the moon he also said the famous words that now define a generation: 'One small step for man, one giant leap for mankind.'

President Kennedy made a vision statement at the beginning of the 1960s for his generation. He declared that, by the decade's end, the United States would have an American walk on the moon. This vision for the country boosted morale as well as creating a surge of growth for the neophyte space programme. With Kennedy's vision, NASA took off and became a dominant force, with all eyes looking at the moon, wondering, 'Can we really do it?'

When Neil Armstrong's foot landed on the moon's surface, it was an evolutionary step for humanity. It showed that anything is possible and it all starts with a vision.

VISION AND GOALS

This is from *Alice in Wonderland*, when Alice first encounters the Cheshire cat in Wonderland. It's a wonderful demonstration of the fact that without goals, or any idea of what you really want or where you are going, you are a bit like Alice, wandering aimlessly throughout life.

'Would you tell me, please, which way I ought to go from here?'

'That depends a good deal on where you want to get to', said the Cat.

'I don't much care where', said Alice.

'Then it doesn't matter which way you go', said the Cat.

'So long as I get somewhere', Alice added as an explanation.

'Oh, you're sure to do that', said the Cat, 'If you only walk long enough.'

Your brain is a goal-seeking mechanism and your ability to set goals is your master skill because goals can unlock your positive mind and release energies and ideas for success and achievement. Without goals, you simply drift and flow on the currents of life. With goals, you fly like an arrow, straight and true to your target. Setting goals will give you direction, purpose and focus in your life.

This is your life

I think the saddest words that anyone could ever say when they look back on their life are 'if only'. You may even catch yourself saying from time to time 'Someday I'll . . .' No one will ever be rich enough to buy back their past. Life is right now and taking action and making things happen is key.

I think there is something, more important than believing: Action! The world is full of dreamers, there aren't enough who will move ahead and begin to take concrete steps to actualize their vision.

W. Clement Stone

Life balance

Looking at creating balance in your life as part of your vision is really important and too much focus on one area won't ensure a smooth ride. The different areas in your life that you may want to consider, for example, are the different roles that you play: husband/wife, father/mother, manager, colleague, team member, sports player, community leader, or friend. Other areas of your life that are important to you may be about your attitude, creative expression, education, family, friends, financial freedom, physical challenge, pleasure, or community service. Having a balance of goals in all areas will give you a well-rounded perspective when you start creating your vision and setting yourself goals to get you to where you really want to be.

The benefits of setting goals

- **Achieve clarity.** Setting goals requires you to develop and gain clarity. This is the first and most important step to creating a life that you want and will help you to establish your personal vision.
- **Focused energy.** If you have clear goals and focus on them, you will get more of what you want and less of what you don't want and preserve precious energy.
- **Personal efficiency.** When you get clear about where you want to go, you will be able to set up steps and create positive actions to get you there. This increases your efficiency because you are working on what is really important. When you work on what's important, you will accomplish more than you ever expected.
- **Increased self confidence.** As you set and achieve your goals, you will become more confident in your ability to do what you say and get what you want in life. Success breeds more success and will increase your self-respect.
- **Get results.** Very few people have proper written goals and, according to research, people who do record their goals will accomplish so much more than those who don't.

HOW TO SET GOALS

A common acronym in goal setting is the familiar SMART goals. SMART is used to describe what experts consider to be good goal statements because they contain most of the essential ingredients. Out of all the formulas I have come across for objective and goal-seeking, it is by far the best and the most easy to apply and stick to.

The SMART acronym has several different variations depending on who you ask. However, this is the interpretation I personally favour to keep it simple; and keepings things simple is by far the most effective way to make progress.

S – Specific

M – Measurable

A – Achievable

R – Recorded

T – Timed

How to write SMART goals

Let's take a closer look at each of these components.

Specific

Your SMART goal plan needs to be a clear and specific statement of what you want. The main reason is that your brain behaves as a goal-seeking mechanism, similar to a precision guided missile. As these missiles fly, they continually make small adjustments and corrections to their trajectories to realign themselves to their target.

Your brain also works in a similar way. Dr Maxwell Maltz, author of the classic *Psycho-Cybernetics*, said that human beings have a built-in, goal-seeking 'success mechanism' that is part of the subconscious mind. This success mechanism is constantly search-ing for ways to help us reach our targets and find answers to our problems. According to Maltz, we work and feel better when our success mechanism is fully engaged going after clear targets. All we have to do to use this mechanism is to give it a specific target. Without one, our success mechanism lies dormant, or worse, pursues targets we didn't consciously choose. When your target is vague or ambiguous, your success mechanism can become confused and either shut down or go after the wrong target.

Measurable

There is an old saying, 'What gets measured gets done'. Making your goal measurable helps you see your progress, recognize if you are moving in the right direction, and see how far you still need to go. Some types of goals, like saving a certain amount of money each month, or reading ten pages a day, or reducing your calorie intake, are very easy to measure, while other goals are not always measurable directly.

For example, if your goal is to improve your relationship with one of your colleagues, how do you measure it? One option is to use some sort of rating. For example, you could say that your relation-ship is a 6 and your goal is to make it an 8. The problem is that these types of ratings are very subjective, can change from day to day, and don't really give you very good feedback. A better option would be to focus your goal on specific actions that you can take that will help you achieve your overall objective.

Achievable

This means that the goal really must be achievable and that doesn't mean easy! You just need to make sure that you have a reasonable expectation of achieving it. For short-term targets, your probability of achieving the goal must be at least 80%. Longer term targets could be more of a stretch and have less probability of success because you have more time to develop your skills to achieve it. For your five to ten year vision, you can go for something really big, even if you currently have no idea how to accomplish it.

Recorded

It is really important that you record your goal, writing down exactly what you specifically want to achieve, why you want to achieve it and how you will measure it. Keep the recorded goals visible so you can remind yourself frequently of what you are hoping to achieve. Something that I did a while ago was to create a visionary board, which is a collage of visual images. At the time, I was targeting ten companies that I admired that I really wanted to work with around modern life skills. I have now had experience of working with eight out of ten of them! Another thing to do, which is fun, is to cut out pictures from a magazine with images of things that you want to cultivate into your life: positive images to remind you what you want to achieve.

Timed

For goals that have a natural ending (like outcome goals), establishing a clear deadline for them adds an element of urgency and motivation. The danger if you don't put a time limit on something is that you will keep making excuses.

All goals must be trackable so you can see what your progress is, either in terms of results you are experiencing, or actions you are taking. Tracking your goals helps you determine if you are going in the right direction and make any necessary adjustments along the way. So you see, just like a precision guided missile!

ACHIEVING GOALS

When you have achieved a goal, take the time to enjoy the satisfaction of having done so. Absorb the implications of the goal achievement, and observe the progress you have made towards other goals. If the goal was a significant one, reward yourself! All of this helps you to create your personal vision and build the life you deserve!

With the experience of having achieved this goal, review the rest of your goal plans and ask yourself the following questions:

● Have I achieved the goal too easily? If so, make your next goal more challenging and stretching.

● Has my goal taken a dispiriting length of time to achieve? If so, make the next goal a little less challenging and stretching.

● Have I learnt something that would lead me to change my other goals? If that is the case, do so.

● Have I noticed a deficit in my skills and do I need to set further goals to fix this?

Failure to meet goals does not matter much, as long as you learn from it and it is an opportunity to feed lessons learned back into your goal-setting programme. Remember, too, that your goals will change as time goes on. Adjust them regularly to reflect the growth in your knowledge and experience; and if goals do not hold any attraction any longer, then let them go. You don't have to wear them like a straitjacket!

Goals at work

In the western business world, it is now very common for employees to take a more active role with their manager in creating their own personal and career development plans. When I first encountered this many years ago, the emphasis was more on my training and development and it didn't really involve setting a work goal of any consequence. Empowering individuals in the workplace to become more accountable is now regarded as an essential motivator, and quite rightly so in my view. Engaging people at this fundamental level makes great business sense.

HOW TO CREATE YOUR VISION AND MAKE IT HAPPEN

Well, let's face it: knowledge is a wonderful thing; however, the real power in knowledge is making things happen. Here are a few things that you can do to keep you on track.

- Share your vision with someone close to you, a family member, a close friend, or someone at work who will support you. The moment you share your dreams with other people, you are putting commitment into them and you will have no other choice but to achieve them. A bit like a second conscience.

- Visualize and affirm your goal every morning as soon as you wake up and right before you go to bed. Many people fail to do this because they think that this does not work. If you do this, you will begin to activate your intention positively and you will motivate yourself by visualizing the achievement of your goals. Put your written goals or visionary board/picture beside your bed so that you can look at it before you sleep and after you wake up.

- Take at least three action steps each and every day to make sure that you move closer toward what you want in your life. If you are serious in making your dreams come true, you must take consistent action every day.

- Make it happen because there are three types of people in life. Those that make things happen, those who watch things happen and those who wonder what happened!

Remember, it is what you do after you create your vision that will determine your success. It is all about getting things done and, as long as you take the necessary action, you will achieve results.

It is so easy to give up sometimes; however, persistence is closely linked with discipline, and one feeds off and supports the other in accomplishing your goals.

The classic speech that Winston Churchill made on 29 October, 1941 to the boys at Harrow School encapsulates the determination required in challenging times.

Never, never, in nothing great or small, large or petty, never give in except to convictions of honour and good sense. Never yield to force; never yield to the apparently overwhelming might of the enemy.

Persistence and determination are what will keep you going in times of confusion, or when things are not going the way you want them to. Your persistent drive will be the clear knowledge of what you really want out of life, what matters to you and having a purpose that you can be proud and motivated about. This indeed is the light at the end of the tunnel!

Certainly life can be very challenging and it does seem that some people have more than their fair share of pain to deal with. However, remember it is all relative and, throughout your lifetime, it is inevitable that you will all have to cope with some form of loss and trauma.

Being resilient takes effort and practice. It may well feel sometimes as if you are taking one step forwards and two steps back, almost as if you are doing a little dance with life. The key, however, is to keep moving and not to lose the faith that you can and will pull through if you remain positive and hopeful. The quicker that you can recover and bounce back the better, because life can pass so quickly and this is your golden opportunity to make the best and the most of it.

I believe every human has a finite number of heartbeats. I don't intend to waste any of mine.

Neil Armstrong

Positive steps

1 Decide what is really important to you
2 Consider all the key components of your life
3 Use the SMART acronym to set goals
4 Create a visionary board/picture
5 Dare to dream and strive to be happy

Create a vision – Personal exercise

Create a visionary board by following the steps below:
- Get some scissors, glue and some old magazines.
- Create a collage on a piece of coloured card of visual images that represent what you want to achieve in your life.
- Look at it every day and begin to live your vision.

DESIDERATA – A CREED FOR LIFE

Go placidly amid the noise and the haste, and remember what peace there may be in silence.

***

As far as possible, without surrender, be on good terms with all persons. Speak your truth quietly and clearly; and listen to others,

even to the dull and the ignorant;

they too have their story.

Avoid loud and aggressive persons;

they are vexatious to the spirit.

***

If you compare yourself with others, you may become vain or bitter,

for always there will be greater and lesser persons than yourself.

Enjoy your achievements as well as your plans. Keep interested in your own career, however humble; it is a real possession in the changing fortunes of time.

***

Exercise caution in your business affairs, for the world is full of trickery.

But let this not blind you to what virtue there is;

many persons strive for high ideals,

and everywhere life is full of heroism.

Be yourself. Especially do not feign affection.

Neither be cynical about love,

for in the face of all aridity and disenchantment,

it is as perennial as the grass.

***

Take kindly the counsel of the years, gracefully surrendering the things of youth. Nurture strength of spirit to shield you in sudden misfortune.

But do not distress yourself with dark imaginings. Many fears are born of fatigue and loneliness.

***

Beyond a wholesome discipline, be gentle with yourself.

You are a child of the universe

no less than the trees and the stars;

you have a right to be here.

And whether or not it is clear to you,

no doubt the universe is unfolding as it should.

***

Therefore be at peace with God, whatever you conceive Him to be.

And whatever your labours and aspirations, in the noisy confusion of life, keep peace in your soul.

***

With all its sham, drudgery, and broken dreams, it is still a beautiful world.

Be cheerful. Strive to be happy.

Written in 1927 by Max Ehrmann (1872–1945)

RESILIENCE MATERIALS

40 WAYS TO BOUNCE BACK

When you are feeling low and need a boost here is a selection of tips that will help you to bounce back and be more resilient and positive about your life.

1. List all your accomplishments

Sometimes you just need to remember all the positive things that you have achieved in your life so making a list to remind yourself will give you a confidence boost.

2. Do ten minutes of exercise

Just a quick ten minutes of exercise. Even a quick run up and down stairs, or standing up and stretching and walking about for a bit, will give you an energy boost and get the endorphins going.

3. Find something to give away

If you have something you don't need or use, and it might be something someone else might need or use, give it to them. It will make you feel good.

4. Lift someone else's spirits

You can turn around bad feelings about yourself right away when you channel your energy into making someone feel good about themselves by doing or saying something nice.

5. Phone a friend

Who needs a psychiatrist when you have friends? Friends can be walking, talking tonics and remind you that you are not alone!

6. Write down a goal

Hope is a very important part of being resilient, so set goals and have something to aim for. If you are feeling a bit low, think of something that would like to achieve and create a goal.

7. Relive your best memory

Focus on a wonderful, happy memory and take a few minutes to dwell on it. Go through all of the details and relive the experience in your mind and see how good it makes you feel.

8. Smile

Just the very act of smiling tells your brain that you are happy. So, no matter how you feel, focus on turning the corners of your mouth up and smile.

9. Turn off your computer and connect

Go and find a living, breathing person and interact with them. Just connecting with another person will help you to feel less isolated and they may say something nice to you that will make you feel better.

10. Let someone else decide

Relinquish responsibility to someone else every now and then. If you feel under pressure, sometimes it is good to take the heat out of the situation and let someone else make the decision for you. You don't always have to be in total control!

11. Listen to your self-talk

Stop and really listen to what you are saying to yourself. Be a detached observer and change your words to words of loving kindness.

12. Make an effort

Get dressed up even if you are feeling really low. Although it may feel like a huge effort it will be worthwhile because when you look in the mirror and see an attractive person on the outside you will begin to feel better on the inside.

13. Choose healthy

If you are feeling low, choose to have a healthy day. Eat lots of things you know will boost your energy and eliminate all the toxins.

14. Do something a bit radical

Shake things up a bit and change your routine. Try something different that makes you feel more like a mover and shaker. It will also get you out of any rut you may find yourself in.

15. Create a blog and share some wisdom

Your life experiences will have taught you lots of things, and sharing what you have learnt with others can be useful. Blogging is also a great way to record some of your thoughts, like a public diary.

16. Read something uplifting

To divert your mind from negative thinking, look for something that will inspire and uplift you. Short passages of writing and motivational quotes can be really good.

17. Surprise someone else

Think of something fun and unexpected for someone that you care about. Planning this will lift your spirits and distract you from feeling gloomy.

18. Make things simple

Taking something that appears to be complicated and simplifying it can be very therapeutic. Often things are far more complex than they really need to be.

19. Heal a rift

If you developed a rift with someone, even if you don't feel you are at fault, extend the olive branch and open yourself to healing the rift. Life is too short!

20. Be a mentor

Be that person for someone in your life who could really use your guidance and advice.

21. Make time for family and friends

In the end, what is more important? Make sure that you invest time, every single day, connecting with the people you love through your time, love, and attention.

22. Put yourself first

Make sure you look after yourself so that you have enough energy for others. So often it is easy to run around trying to be everything to everybody and neglect your own needs. Make sure that you take time each day for you to relax and just be.

23. Learn to say no

Avoid being bullied or shamed into doing something you do not want to do. Do not be afraid of saying no thank you.

24. Learn to say yes

Open yourself up to new opportunities and experiences, to new friends and doing things spontaneously. There are so many adventures that you still have yet to embrace.

25. Rest for ten minutes

Stop and rest. Take ten minutes to do absolutely nothing. Close your eyes and allow yourself to just be in the moment. Cat napping can work wonders!

26. Breathe deeply

Learn a proper breathing technique and take time each day, especially if you feel stressed, to focus on your breathing. It is healing for the body and mind.

27. Get a mini massage

Ask someone you feel comfortable with to massage your shoulders. A loving touch will remind you that you are connected to others and that your physical happiness is important.

28. Be present right now

Stop dwelling on the past or worrying about the future. Focus on the here and now. See it. Hear it. Feel it. Taste it. Touch it. Sense it in every way that you can.

29. Pay a bill

If you have outstanding bills that need to be paid then sort it out now. The energy and stress of them hanging over your head will pull you into a hole and you will feel better once it is done.

30. Watch a funny film

Watching an uplifting and funny film or show is a good way to pick your spirits up and absorb you in something a bit lighthearted for a while. There is nothing wrong with a little bit of escapism.

31. Listen to uplifting music

There are some great pieces of music and songs that can really make you feel better. Songs that you can sing along to with positive lyrics work really well.

32. Drink water

Drink a large glass of water. This will rehydrate you, will flush out all the unwanted toxins and give you more energy.

33. Take the first steps

When you feel overwhelmed, remember every journey begins with the first step. Break it down. Start in a small way, one step at a time and carry on.

34. Keep a thought journal

A good way to release anxieties and worries is to write them down. This will help you to be able to put them into perspective and tangibly take hold of what is worrying you and work out how you can turn it around.

35. Have a nice cup of tea

A nice cup of chamomile tea with a tiny bit of honey can be very comforting. Sit quietly and sip your tea and just enjoy the experience which will be pleasant and soothing.

36. Plan a party

Parties are fun and people like people who organize parties. It doesn't have to be a huge affair. Just get fun people together for a drink or a meal or a picnic.

37. Look upwards and outwards

When you feel down it is usually where you will be looking! So lift your head up and look upwards and outwards. Noticing the world and everything around you will make you feel ten times better.

38. Compliment someone

Just say something nice to someone that you notice about them. Make someone else's day with your words, and it will make yours.

39. Plan your day

This is something that works so well. Plan and prioritize three things that you know you want to achieve. Plan them in the morning or the night before and see what you have accomplished each day. This will make you feel very positive and give you a great big boost.

40. Do highlights

At the end of the day identify three things that were the best bits of your day. Share them with your partner, family or friends or just record them in a diary. Doing this before you go to sleep will help you to feel better about yourself and your life in general and will help you to be more positive and resilient.

TOP 20 SURVIVAL SONGS

When you are feeling really low, one of the best ways to lift your spirits is to listen to some uplifting music. Here is my top twenty list of survival songs, which will help you through some of those times.

1. Nat King Cole – Smile

2. Gloria Gaynor – I Will Survive

3. Florence & the Machine – You Got the Love

4. Gabrielle – Rise

5. Mike Oldfield – Heaven's Open

6. Diana Ross – I'm Coming Out

7. U2 – Stuck in a Moment

8. Sugababes – Stronger

9. Fleetwood Mac – Don't Stop

10. Shirley Bassey – I am What I am

11. Chumbawamba – Tubthumping

12. Ultravox – One Small Day

13. Gerry Rafferty – Get It Right Next Time

14. D B Boulevard – Point of View

15. Yazz – The Only Way is Up

16. M People – Reach for the Hero

17. Monty Python – Always Look on the Bright Side of Life

18. Kim Appleby – Don't Worry

19. ABBA – I Have a Dream

20. Vera Lynn – White Cliffs of Dover

USEFUL RESOURCES

There are so many excellent resources that can help you to develop your life skills. Here are some recommended sources which I have found extremely useful and inspiring.

BOOKS

Psycho-Cybernetics, Maxwell Maltz

SUMO, Paul McGee

Mind Power, James Borg

Change Your Life with CBT, Corinne Sweet

Change Your Thinking – Change Your Life, Brian Tracy

Happiness, Richard Layard

Learned Optimism, Martin Seligman

Motivate to Win, Richard Denny

Six Thinking Hats, Edward de Bono

Assertiveness and Diversity, Anni Townend

The Extraordinary Reader, Clive Lewis and Anthony Landale

Meditation – The stress solution, Mary Pearson

The Happiness Purpose, Edward de Bono

Dare to Live Without Limits, Bryan Golden

Succeed for Yourself, Richard Denny

Wellbeing, Cary Cooper and Ivan Robertson

Learning to Think Strategically, Julia Stone

The A–Z of Good Mental Health, Jeremy Thomas and Dr Tony Hughes

Wet Mind: The New Cognitive Neuroscience, Stephen Michael Kosslyn and Olivier Koenig

Other titles by Liggy Webb are available on Amazon and in all good book shops

How to Be Happy – Simple ways to build your confidence and resilience to become a happier healthier you

How to Work Wonders – Your Guide to Workplace Wellness

Thank you – Your Guide to Appreciating Life

Modern Life Skills – A compendium of 20 key life skills

Also add email info@liggywebb.com for a free mini e sample of How To Be Happy

WEBSITES

MIND

www.mind.org.uk

MIND provides advice and support to empower anyone experiencing a mental health problem, and campaigns to improve services, raise awareness and promote understanding.

MentalHelp.net

www.mentalhelp.net (select 'Emotional Resilience' from the Topic List dropdown)

The Mental Help Net website exists to promote online mental health education and provides scientifically accurate and up-to-date coverage of mental health and illness topics. The site's resources take three different forms. It offers detailed and comprehensive coverage of mental health and illness topics (such as Depression, ADHD and Personality Disorders) in numerous topic centres. It regularly publishes original blogs, podcasts, articles and advice columns, and offers a Mental Health Support Community. The service is freely available and intended for both laypeople and professionals.

American Psychological Association

www.apa.org

The American Psychological Association is the world's largest association of psychologists. Its mission is to advance the creation, communication and application of psychological knowledge to benefit society and improve people's lives.

NHS Choices: Mental Health

www.nhs.uk

NHS Choices is the UK's biggest health website. It provides a comprehensive health information service that puts you in control of your healthcare.

Living Life to the Full

www.llttf.com

A course written by a psychiatrist who has many years of experience using a Cognitive Behaviour Therapy (CBT) approach and also in helping people use these skills in everyday life. During the development phase of the course, each module has been used by a wide range of health care practitioners and members of the public.

Business in the Community

ww.bitc.org.uk

This Emotional Resilience Toolkit provides practical guidance in promoting the resilience of individuals and teams in companies as part of an integrated health and well-being programme.

YoungMinds

www.youngminds.org.uk

YoungMinds is the UK's leading charity, committed to improving the emotional well-being and mental health of children and young people. Driven by their experiences, they campaign, research and influence policy and practice.

Action for Happiness

www.actionforhappiness.org

Action for Happiness is a movement for positive social change. It aims to bring together people from all walks of life who want to play a part in creating a happier society for everyone. I strongly recommend that you register and join the movement. It will positively change your life as well as benefitting others at the same time!

My website

www.liggywebb.com

I had to mention this one because there is a whole range of free, downloadable materials, all geared to help promote health and happiness. Please visit and take advantage of what is on offer. This also includes electronic personal action plans that will help you to set goals and track results.

ACKNOWLEDGEMENTS

There is an endless list of people I would like to thank for helping me make this book happen. So, huge thanks to all my family and friends, to all the members of The Learning Architect, The Montpellier Writers Group and to all my colleagues at The United Nations.

There are four people who deserve a very special mention for getting me out of my dark rabbit hole of semantics whilst writing this book. Lawrence Mcilhoney, Melanie Lisney, author Peter Stone and Andrew Wylde (to whom I must credit the term Doomerang!)

Special thanks to Jenny Ng, for her inspiring and encouraging editing; and everyone at Capstone Wiley for being such a great publisher to work with.

And thank you to all the people I have met along the way, who have allowed me to share their stories, and who have inspired me with their strength and courage.

ABOUT THE
AUTHOR

Liggy Webb is widely respected as a specialist in the field of Modern Life Skills. As a presenter, consultant and author, she is passionate about her work and improving the quality of people's lives. She has researched and developed a range of techniques and strategies, to support individuals and organizations to cope more effectively and successfully with the demands and challenges of modern living.

Liggy is noted for her dynamic and engaging style and, as a result, is frequently invited to present and speak at international conferences, award ceremonies, on board cruise ships, in the media and at a variety of high profile events. Her website, www. liggywebb.com, offers a range of downloadable complimentary toolkits and materials.

Liggy is an international consultant for the United Nations and travels extensively, working in a variety of worldwide locations. She is also the founding director of The Learning Architect (www. thelearningarchitect.com), an international learning and development organization based in the UK. In her spare time, Liggy runs a creative writing group in her home town, Cheltenham, and is currently working on a fiction book, about which she is feeling very excited!

INDEX

accomplishments, listing your 151
action plans 71, 78, 85–6
adaptability xii–xiii, xviii, 52
alcohol xix, 91, 101, 123–4
'amiable' personality 63, 67
amnesia 50–1
'analytical' personality 66–7
anger 32, 34, 36, 54, 62, 69, 72
anxiety 77, 91, 96, 111, 130
    change as cause of 52–3
    influence of caffeine on 95, 124–5
    mindfulness as remedy for 97
    triggered by stress 41, 93
apologising 28
appreciation, showing 106, 110
Aristotle 109, 133
Armstrong, Neil 134, 135, 144
assertiveness 94

Bach, Richard 47
balance, work-life 98–101, 107–8, 136–7
blogging 154
brain processes 24–6, 139
Branden, Nathaniel 3
breathing techniques 42, 97, 156
Buddha 62, 122

caffeine 91, 94–5, 101, 124–5
calmness 57, 58, 70
cancer 20–3
carbohydrates 43, 91, 101
change 47–59
    anger management 72
    grief cycle model 54
    positive thinking xviii, 19
    self-awareness 14
Churchill, Winston xx, 117, 118, 143
comedians 128–9
communication 65–6, 68, 71, 85, 94

compassion 32, 36, 63, 105
compliments, giving 12, 113, 158
compulsive spending 124
conflict xviii, 61–73
    benefits of 64–6
    coping with 69–73
    definition of 63
    personality types 66–8
Confucius xi
'controlling the controllables' 119, 122–31
'Cool Down' model 71, 73
coping mechanisms 24, 45
    dealing with conflict 69–73
    healthy 125–6, 131
    unhealthy xii, 44, 123–4
creativity 19, 78, 79–83, 87

Darwin, Charles 38, 52
De Bono, Edward 81
decision making 19, 83–6, 87, 153
depression 33, 35–6, 43, 44, 90, 111, 130
    grief cycle model 54
    influence of caffeine on 95, 124–5
    mindfulness as remedy for 97
    triggered by stress 41, 94
Desiderata – A Creed for Life 29, 128,
    147–9
desire 8
determination xx, 118–20, 143–4
diet 43–4, 89, 91, 101, 123, 153
'driver' personality 63, 66, 67

eating, emotional 123
Edison, Thomas A. 63
Einstein, Albert xxi
Eliot, George 15
Emotional Freedom Therapy (EFT)
    126
emotional intelligence 13, 38–41, 44, 45

emotions 31–45
　during change 53, 56, 59
　conflict triggering 68, 69
　control over xvii–xviii, 70, 72
　food linked with 43–4
　grief cycle model 54
　how to manage 42
　purpose of 37–8
　repressing 57
　'thinking hats' 81
　understanding 34–7, 44, 45
empathy 13, 32, 39, 41, 71, 107
environmental stress 93
excuses 28, 29
exercise xix, 12, 42, 89, 90–1, 95, 101, 151
'expressive' personality 66, 67
externally-referenced people 4–5

family xix, 100, 104, 105–8, 114, 142, 155
fear 8, 44, 69, 148
feedback 5, 9, 14, 78
flexibility xviii, 56
food 43–4, 91, 101, 123, 153
friends xix, 100, 104, 109–10, 114, 142, 152, 155

Gandhi, Mahatma 73
generosity 32, 110
Gibran, Khalil 25
Gilbert, Elizabeth 31
giving 62, 104, 151
goals xx, 133, 135–42, 143, 144, 152
　problem solving 77, 78, 87
　reticular activating system 26
Goleman, Daniel 38
gratitude 12, 110, 113
grief cycle model 54

happiness 6, 33, 107, 111, 113–14, 149, 156
health xix, 41, 89–102
　food 43–4, 91, 101, 123, 153
　immune system 18
　NHS website 165
　positive thinking 19
　relaxation 95–8
　self-confidence 12
　smoking 124
　stress 92–5

　work-life balance 98–101
　see also mental health
highlights 159
hobbies 100
holidays 100
humour 108, 128–30

immune system 18
inspiration 127–8, 131
internal dialogue 24, 26, 29
internal stress 93
internally-referenced people 4
investment in yourself 9–10

Jordan, Michael 130–1
journals 42, 158

'Keep Calm and Carry On' 57, 58
Kennedy, John F. 134–5
kindness 32, 110, 112, 113
King, Martin Luther 17, 103
Kübler-Ross, Elizabeth 54

Lao-tzu 10
laughter 129–30, 157
leading by example 112–13
learning from mistakes 27–8, 29
Lennon, John 114
letting go 91, 95, 120–2, 131
life balance 98–101, 107–8, 136–7
limits, setting 99–100
listening to others 65, 71
love 32, 110, 114, 148, 155
Lucado, Max 61

Maltz, Dr Maxwell 139
Mandela, Nelson 19
Maslow, Abraham 86
Mayer, John 38
McGee, Paul 121
meaning, finding 112
memories, reliving 152
mental health 41, 43–4, 90, 96, 125, 164–5
　see also health
mentoring 155
Milne, A. A. 1
mind over matter 24–7
mindfulness 97–8

mistakes 11, 27–8, 29
mobile technology 100
mood 41, 42, 43, 72
motivation 39, 71, 134, 143
music 96–7, 128, 157, 161–2

negative baggage xii, xx, 120–2, 126, 131
negative emotions 18, 32, 34, 40
Neuro-Linguistic Programming 4
nutrition *see* diet

omega-3 oils 43–4
open-mindedness 14, 33, 53, 55–6, 59, 156
opportunities xviii–xix, 59, 76, 86, 87
  see also proportunities
optimism xvii, 18, 19–20, 134
  dealing with cancer 20–3
  how to be optimistic 23–4
  learning opportunities 27–8
  mind over matter 24–7
  'thinking hats' 81, 82
  see also positive thinking
outward focus 12–13, 158

pain 42, 144
parties 158
Peale, Norman Vincent 75
perseverance xii–xiii, xx, 118–20, 143–4
personal responsibility 2, 6, 23, 24, 29, 55, 59, 112
personality xii, 63, 66–8, 72
perspective, challenging your 57
pessimism xvii, 23, 82
physical appearance 12, 153
physical health *see* health
planning 58, 78, 159
positive thinking xiii, xvii, 18, 19–20, 26–7
  change xviii, 53, 56, 59
  emotions 33, 34
  see also optimism
posture 11
problem solving xix, 19, 76–9, 83
proportunities xviii–xix, 75–87
  creativity 79–83
  decision making 83–6
  problem-solving process 76–9
psychometric tests 66

psychoneuroimmunology 18
purpose, connecting to your 111–12, 114

redundancies 36–7
referencing systems 4–5
relationships
  emotional intelligence 41
  empathy 39
  optimism 19
  resilience and 110–11
  social skills 40
  strengthened by conflict 68, 69
  trust 9
  see also family; friends
relaxation 82–3, 91, 95–8, 100, 101, 155
respect 108, 113
  see also self-respect
rest 156
  see also relaxation
reticular activating system (RAS) 25–6
risk taking 82, 84–5

Salovey, Peter 38
self-awareness xvii, 13–14, 38–9, 55
self-confidence xvii, 10–13, 14, 23, 39, 137
self-control xvii–xviii, 33, 39
self-discovery xvii, 2–15, 65
self-esteem 3, 4, 7–8, 13, 48, 68
self-fulfilling prophecies 24, 69, 94
self-love 7
self-perception 5
self-regulation 39
self-respect 2, 23
self-talk 26, 29, 153
self-worth 2, 7–8, 13, 110
Serenity Prayer 122
serotonin 43, 95, 130
simplicity 154
sleep xix, 96, 97, 98
SMART goals 137–41, 144
smiling 128–30, 152
smoking 124
social connections xix, 103–15, 153
  see also relationships
social skills 40
social support 42, 57, 126, 130
speaking up 12
Stone, W. Clement 136

strengths xvii, 2, 11, 14, 15, 39, 106
stress xii, 41, 42, 71, 111
    bringing stress home 100–1, 107, 108
    caffeine impact on 124–5
    change as cause of 53
    decision making 83
    diet impact on 43
    emotional eating 123
    exercise impact on 90
    letting go of 91
    managing 70, 82, 92–5
    poor communication leading to 68
    relaxation and 95, 96
    repressing emotions 57
    smoking and 124
    workplace 36–7
success 5, 6, 130–1, 137, 139
support 42, 57, 126, 130
survival songs 161–2
survival stress 92
sympathy 23, 71

talking to people 42, 57
tapping 126
tea, drinking 158

'thinking hats' 81–2
thinking time 99
Thoreau, Henry David 59
time management 94
Tolstoy, Leo 55
trauma xii, 19, 48–51, 123, 144
trust 9, 68, 69

uncertainty 53, 83
Urich, Robert 101

values xviii, 63, 68
valuing yourself 6–8, 14
victim mentality 23–4, 29
vision xx, 133–45
visualization 26, 118, 119, 142–3

water xix, 91, 101, 157
weaknesses 2, 14, 15, 39, 106
websites 164–7
well-being xi, xix, 90, 99, 107
Wilde, Oscar 45
work-life balance 98–101, 107–8, 136–7
workplace situations 4–5, 36–7, 40–1, 93,
    142